The Columbine
High School
Massacre

PERSPECTIVES ON

The Columbine High School Massacre
Murder in the Classroom

KATIE MARSICO

Marshall Cavendish
Benchmark
New York

Other Marshall Cavendish Offices: Marshall Cavendish International (Asia) Private Limited, 1 New Industrial Road, Singapore 536196 • Marshall Cavendish International (Thailand) Co Ltd. 253 Asoke, 12th Flr, Sukhumvit 21 Road, Klongtoey Nua, Wattana, Bangkok 10110, Thailand • Marshall Cavendish (Malaysia) Sdn Bhd, Times Subang, Lot 46, Subang Hi-Tech Industrial Park, Batu Tiga, 40000 Shah Alam, Selangor Darul Ehsan, Malaysia

Marshall Cavendish is a trademark of Times Publishing Limited

All websites were available and accurate when this book was sent to press.

Library of Congress Cataloging-in-Publication Data

Marsico, Katie, 1980–
The Columbine High School massacre: murder in the classroom / by Katie Marsico.
p. cm. — (Perspectives on)
Includes bibliographical references and index.
Summary: "Provides comprehensive information on the Columbine High School massacre and the examination of violence in schools"—Provided by publisher.
ISBN 978-0-7614-4985-0
1. Columbine High School (Littleton, Colo.) 2. Columbine High School Massacre, Littleton, Colo., 1999. 3. School violence—Colorado. 4. School violence—United States—Prevention. 5. Students—Crimes against—United States—Prevention. I. Title.
LB3013.33.C6M37 2010
373.17'820978882—dc22
2009020590

Editor: Christine Florie
Publisher: Michelle Bisson
Art Director: Anahid Hamparian
Series Designer: Sonia Chaghatzbanian
Expert Reader: Dr. Jeffrey R. Sprague, associate professor of special education and codirector, University of Oregon Institute on Violence and Destructive Behavior, University of Oregon, Eugene

Photo research by Marybeth Kavanagh

Cover photo by Michael Smith/Getty Images

The photographs in this book are used by permission and through the courtesy of: *Getty Images*: 47; James Keivom, 2–3; Jeff Haynes/AFT, 8; Jefferson County Sherriff's Dept., 23, 37; Kevin Moloney, 55; Tim Boyle, 81; Marc Piscotty, 89; *Reuters Pictures*/Ho New, 15L, 15R; *AP Photo*: HO, 19, 35; Ed Andrieski, 40; Jefferson County Sherriff, 60; Green Bay Police Dept., 75; *Everett Collection*: Rex USA, 30, 67.

Printed in Malaysia (T)
1 3 5 6 4 2

Contents

Introduction

FOR THE STUDENTS AND STAFF MEMBERS at Columbine High School, residents of Littleton, Colorado, and Americans across the country, April 20, 1999, was a date that would remain infamous for years to come. At 11:19 a.m., eighteen-year-old Eric Harris and seventeen-year-old Dylan Klebold began a shooting rampage at the school that would ultimately result in their own suicides, the deaths of twelve students and one teacher, and injuries to twenty-three others. Yet far more trauma was incurred than can be measured by body counts.

The Columbine massacre forced the nation to examine school violence as it never had before and to accept the reality that if such an episode could rock the quiet suburb of Littleton, similar occurrences had the potential to shatter lives anywhere. Though numb from shock and horror, U.S. citizens also responded to the killings by questioning what could have driven two teenagers to commit murder. They subsequently analyzed a multitude of possibilities, including bullying in the classroom and violence in the media.

Americans explored various perspectives on the tragedy, whether the Columbine massacre could have been prevented, and ways to stop similar incidents from taking place. By sharing their thoughts on topics ranging from gun control to threat evaluation and student profiling, everyone from average teens to psychology experts used the rampage as a framework for examining the broader issue of school violence. Analyzing how school shootings that took place after Columbine were similar to that massacre also helped the country to better understand both what prompts such destruction and what might help deter it.

More than a decade after Harris and Klebold wreaked havoc on their community, the nation continues to struggle with the tragedy that was the Columbine killings. Fortunately, however, Americans also study the event and use it to inform their perspectives on school violence. It is through these differing and sometimes controversial thoughts and vantage points that people of all backgrounds have united since the massacre to try to better comprehend what happened that day and to attempt to eradicate violence from the country's classrooms.

One

School Violence That Left Society Shaken

ON THE MORNING OF APRIL 20, 1999, sixteen-year-old Nicole Nowlen finished geometry class at Columbine High School in Littleton, Colorado, which is located in Jefferson County, about 14 miles south of Denver. Heading to the library so she could focus on her homework, she initially sensed nothing particularly unusual about the cool spring morning and went about her business with approximately two thousand of her fellow students. It was only after Nowlen took a seat in the library shortly after 11:00 a.m. that she became aware of anything out of the ordinary. "At about 11:20 a.m., a girl came running down the hall and into the library screaming, 'Help! Help! There are some people downstairs with guns!'" she recalled a few days later.

> She proceeded to find one of the librarians to call 911, and we just sat at our tables just all looking at each other. I personally thought it was a senior prank to scare all of us and thought nothing of it. A few seconds later,

Students grieve at a candlelight vigil held on April 21, 1999, one day after the killing of fifteen people and injuring of twenty-three others at Columbine High School.

a boy came in with a gunshot wound to
his leg. I still then thought it was a prank
because you couldn't see if [his] leg was hurt
or not. A teacher or librarian was on the
phone with the police and was telling us to
get under the tables in case [the shooters]
came in. She was very frantic on the
phone and kept yelling at us, which got me
worrying that this wasn't a joke.

Then we heard guns going off
in the cafeteria below us and people
screaming and running. The screaming
later stopped, and then they were setting
off bombs or explosives below us. The
whole building shook, and I was having a
real hard time keeping myself calm. During
all of this, somehow the fire alarm came
on, and it had a real high shrill ringing to
it. I [was] looking at other people around
me when I saw one of the gunmen walk by
a window by the door. He had on a black
trench coat, black hat, and blonde curly hair
that hung down to his chin. I later found
out that this was Dylan Klebold.

I started whispering to the guy at the
table next to me what I had just seen go past
the window. . . . I whispered again to the guy
next to me if I could hide with him because
his table was at a different angle to the door,
and you wouldn't see us under the table. He
motioned for me to come over, and I crawled

on the floor, got up against one of the sides
under the table, and we pulled the chairs in
around us to form a barrier. As he sat across
from me, the first thing he did was take a
hold of my hand, and we just sat quietly . . .
hoping they wouldn't come in. A few minutes
passed, and in they came. The first thing they
told us was for everyone to get out. No one
moved. I mean . . . what do you do? Attempt
to get up and walk out and get shot in the
back, or do you wait to get shot while you're
cornered under a table?

I don't remember too much of what
was said in the library because I was just
holding his hand and looking at him the whole
time. . . . Then we saw black combat boots
next to our table, and then a gun was pointed
under it and was fired two times. We didn't
scream but moved away as far as we could.
The table was next to one of the shelves of
books built into the wall, so you could still sort
of hide on the other side but still be safe under
the table. I stayed partway under the table,
and the boy came out from under it. That is
when they shot him again, and I thought he
had died because his leg was touching mine,
and you could feel him start to shake like
[he was having] a seizure.

I then sat as still as I could . . . hoping
he would think I was dead. [The shooter]
then asked me, 'Are you still breathing?' I

> didn't say anything. . . . I just laid down sort
> of out of instinct. I laid down and closed my
> eyes, hoping he would think I was dead and
> wouldn't shoot me anymore. I then blacked
> out. I didn't dream or see my life flash before
> my eyes, but it was a quiet black.

Though she probably didn't realize it as she lapsed into darkness, Nowlen was among the lucky ones that day. The commotion she had at first believed to be a senior prank was, in fact, the makings of the Columbine massacre—a killing spree led by students Eric Harris and Dylan Klebold that raised public awareness of school violence to new heights. Within less than an hour the pair committed atrocities that culminated in fifteen deaths, including their own suicides, and the injury of twenty-three other people.

While the perpetrators were largely recognized as introverted social outcasts, few of the teens' acquaintances and teachers suspected that they would choose April 20, 1999, to roam the halls of Columbine armed with an arsenal that included semiautomatic weapons and homemade pipe bombs, wounding and slaying any unlucky individuals who couldn't flee in time to seek adequate cover. At some point in their young lives, though, Harris and Klebold made a terrifying transformation. The pair proved to be the masterminds behind one of the most savage incidents of school violence in U.S. history.

Years after the infamous Columbine massacre, people from psychologists to law-enforcement officials to survivors continue to ponder why such tragedies occur and how they can be prevented. Their perspectives on school violence all

It Could Happen Here

The Columbine massacre was by no means America's first school shooting. In fact, there were four episodes of school violence that claimed a total of nine lives in 1998 alone. That said, however, experts classify the Littleton killings as distinct because of the extent of the carnage that occurred, as well as the perpetrators' terrifying level of premeditation. Just as important, however, the Columbine incident completely shattered whatever faith Americans had in the idea that gunfire and death only plagued urban, inner-city schools.

"It was no longer possible to disassociate—'Oh, that's something that happened at some faraway town in some other state,'" explained Glenn Muschert, an associate professor of sociology at Miami University in Oxford, Ohio, during a 2009 interview intended to commemorate Columbine's tenth anniversary. "People started to have the perception that 'It could happen here.'"

play a significant role in determining the circumstances and sequence of happenings that led up to April 20, 1999, and the young men's forty-nine-minute rampage. With luck, this understanding will prevent similar occurrences from plaguing other campuses and taking additional lives.

Closeted Killers

In April 1999 Harris and Klebold were due to graduate from Columbine within a matter of weeks. Harris indicated that he would enlist in the U.S. Marine Corps; Klebold was making plans to attend the University of Arizona in Tucson. From the perspective of several of their friends, family members, and acquaintances, both young men seemed to be leading fairly normal existences in the meantime, even if they couldn't exactly be classified as members of the social mainstream. And, from what most people knew of them, this pattern didn't deviate from their norm.

Harris and his family—father Wayne Harris, mother Kathy Pool Harris, and older brother Kevin Harris—had settled in Littleton in 1993 after several moves between military bases across the country to accommodate Wayne's career as a transport pilot for the U.S. Air Force. Not long after taking up residence in Colorado, the former serviceman was forced to pursue a new career working for a flight-safety corporation due to military cutbacks, while Kathy found employment as a caterer.

Harris met Klebold during junior high at Ken Caryl Middle School, and the two quickly became good friends. Unlike Harris, Klebold had spent all of his early life in Colorado. His father, Thomas Klebold, a geophysicist, and

Though seemingly leading normal lives, Harris (left) and Klebold (right) had a reputation as outcasts at Columbine High School.

his mother, Susan Yassenoff Klebold, an employment counselor. The couple also had an older son, named Byron.

From an early age Klebold showed a great aptitude for academics and was even briefly enrolled in a program for gifted elementary school students. By the time he and Harris were introduced to one another at Ken Caryl, it was clear that both boys were intelligent, thoughtful adolescents. They shared a deep interest in such activities as playing computer games and creating video productions and belonged to a small circle of friends that included classmate Brooks Brown.

Yet beyond this limited group of acquaintances, Harris and Klebold earned a reputation for being outside the social mainstream. Once the pair began attending Columbine High School in 1995, this lack of acceptance was compounded when they faced what many former students described as a clique-filled environment that often rendered teenagers who weren't extremely popular or athletic an easy target for bullies. Harris and Klebold were not complete outcasts, as they held jobs at a local pizza parlor called Blackjack Pizza and contributed to Columbine's Rebel News Network and the maintenance of the school computer server. That said, none of their classmates mistook them for members of the "in" crowd. The friends harbored bizarre interests in Nazism, a violent computer game called *Doom*, and discussions that frequently revolved around weapons and explosive devices.

Unsurprisingly, many of the students who were familiar with Harris and Klebold regarded such fascinations as somewhat odd, but most wrote them off as no more than the eccentricities of two misfits who were impressed by military culture and technology. In fact, years later, several classmates remembered them as neither vicious killers nor pitiable victims of bullying, but described each as initially appearing to be a "normal guy" or a "typical kid." Columbine attendee Jennifer LaPlante recalled after the massacre how Harris in particular never gave her any reason to suspect that he was even capable of such violence. "I think he was the greatest actor I've ever known," she confessed in May 1999. "He never . . . deviated from the character I knew—a bright, smiling kid."

As Harris's and Klebold's time at Columbine went on, however, clues to how unhappy the young men truly were began to manifest themselves in a variety of ways. A handful of individuals started to recognize two individuals who were anything but bright and smiling.

Culture of the Crime Scene and Signs of Trouble

Twenty-five years old in the spring of 1999, Columbine proudly claimed the motto "The finest kids in America pass through these halls"and had undergone major improvements and renovations in 1995. With almost two thousand individuals enrolled at the time of the massacre, the institution also boasted impressive graduation and attendance rates and offered a variety of extracurricular clubs and sports activities. Like most other high schools, however, the Littleton institution was not free from cliques, and social acceptance was not a commodity to be taken for granted. As Brown's father later attested, his son and Harris and Klebold "were outcasts, kids who didn't fit in."As he further explained of Columbine, "It is a school of cliques and the athletes [were] the biggest, toughest group."

Realizing that they weren't members of the mainstream, Harris and Klebold gradually began to develop an intense and abnormal hatred for anyone who was. "I want to burn the world, I want to kill everyone except [for] about five people," Harris professed in his journal in 1998. A similar rant read as follows: "You know what I hate? MANKIND!!!! Kill everything. . . . Kill everything." Klebold's admissions from about this time were equally disturbing. "The lonely man strikes with absolute rage," he scribbled in a day planner.

What, society continues to wonder years later, prompted these young men—and the perpetrators of other episodes of school violence—to devolve into killers? In addition to their obvious lack of mental stability, did bullying at school trigger Harris's and Klebold's transition, or were wider-reaching outside factors, such as violence in the media, to blame? What indications did they give of their brutal intentions, and was there any way that those around them could have foreseen what was coming? The answers to several of these questions continue to be debated, but what remains uncontestable is that Harris's and Klebold's grip on reality, social views, and personal coping mechanisms began to deteriorate as time elapsed.

Once Harris became a sophomore, he grew bolder and more outspoken, often appearing to be the dominant personality in his friendship with Klebold. He didn't even hesitate to challenge the jocks who cut ahead of people in the lunch line, despite the fact that it almost inevitably invited their wrath. Sadly, being thrown against lockers and called names was not an uncommon occurrence at the school, where there was a definite pecking order that separated those who were accepted from those who sat on the fringes.

Harris and Klebold increasingly set themselves apart from the mainstream during their junior year, when they reportedly joined a band of fellow students who called themselves the Trench Coat Mafia. Dressing in long, dark coats often sported by members of a punk subculture known as Goths, the teens in this social niche considered themselves to be outsiders who felt isolated from and abused by certain athletes and other popular Columbine attendees. Some believe that a classmate and coworker at Blackjack inspired Harris and Klebold to latch on to the group, though the association likely only furthered any ridicule they already endured.

Harris (left) and Klebold (right) are believed to have joined a group of students who called themselves the Trench Coat Mafia.

"Everywhere they went, they were taunted and teased about how they dressed," remarked Tiffany Typher, a girl Harris had escorted to the homecoming dance his freshman year. "You could tell [Harris would] get upset by it. What might have driven him to [kill] might have been the way the jocks treated him. If you're called a psycho all your life, you're going to live out that reputation."

Apart from their choice of clothing, additional odd behaviors were later recognized as clues that all was not right with Harris and Klebold. The pair ranted violently

Reflections of a Misfit

Despite some of Klebold's violent and deranged writings, the journal he kept from 1997 to 1999 was not always filled with messages of hate and destruction. On the contrary, several of the entries included romantic themes or were scribbled on pages patterned with etchings of hearts. At the same time, however, the thoughts and confessions Klebold put on paper were often controlled by a sense of sad solitude and estrangement from those around him.

"The framework of society stands above and below me," he penned during high school.

The hardest thing to destroy yet the weakest thing that exists. I know that I am different, yet I am afraid to tell the society. The possible abandonment [and] persecution is not something I want to face, yet it is so primitive to me. I guess being yourself means letting people know about inner thoughts, too, not just opinions and fashions. . . . I will be free one day, in the land of purity and my happiness; I will have a love, someone who is me in a way. Someday . . . possibly thru this life, maybe another, but it will happen. . . .

via everything from handwritten journals and personal Web pages to homemade videos and stories for their creative writing class. They decried classmates whom they regarded as tormenters and even submitted school projects such as the video *Hitmen for Hire*, which depicted students being murdered in the hallways. While teachers were periodically disturbed by these "academic" efforts, Harris and Klebold always were able to convince authority figures that they intended the work as pure fiction.

In the meantime, they failed to stay out of trouble on other fronts. In January 1998 they were arrested when they burglarized a van and stole approximately $400 worth of electronics. But after paying a fine, performing community service, and attending court-mandated anger-management sessions, the teens persuaded officials that they were penitent and suffered no further punishment for the deed.

At Columbine, though, they continued to create the occasional ruckus, sometimes using their access to the school's server to obtain the locker combinations of classmates they considered enemies or stealing various pieces of computer equipment. Despite the fact that these incidents didn't bring about serious long-term consequences for Harris or Klebold, a dean of students once observed how he perceived in the pair "the potential for an 'evil side'" and went on to aptly prophesize "that there was a violent, angry streak in these kids."

The teens' preoccupation with weapons did little to contradict this assessment. Forever fascinated with bombs, Harris and Klebold periodically found themselves in trouble with management at Blackjack for bringing homemade incendiary devices to work or for setting small fires behind the restaurant. Again, however, few people considered such

Harris (left) and Klebold (right) practice firing a gun at a makeshift shooting range on March 6, 1999.

incidents to be more than annoying examples of mischief-making and boys being boys.

Eventually, Brown's parents were forced to view Harris's and Klebold's behavior as something more sinister. In 1998 Harris began threatening the Browns' son after the friends had a falling-out. Though Harris initially apologized to the family, they were later tipped off to numerous menacing messages on Harris's personal Web page that specifically referenced Brown. Brown's parents contacted authorities and claimed after the massacre that officials did little to pursue the matter, despite the fact that the website also mentioned how Harris had been creating and detonating his own pipe bombs. Following the killings Jefferson County law enforcement responded to these accusations with various excuses, many of which indicated that they believed a slightly eccentric teen was making mischief rather than doing something that would pose a risk to those around him.

Either way, Harris and Klebold managed to avoid intense scrutiny once more—scrutiny that might have alerted authorities to the possibility that they would act on their threats. And as the pair progressed through the latter half of their academic career at Columbine, their daydreams of mass killing did indeed transform into carefully calculated plans. All Harris and Klebold needed to do was formulate a specific strategy for murder and obtain the necessary weapons. Then, shortly before graduation, they would be able to orchestrate destruction so unforgettable that it would force people across the nation to examine and analyze school violence as they never had before.

Two

April 20, 1999

TO THE OUTSIDE WORLD HARRIS AND KLEBOLD may have ranged in appearance from quirky, counterculture teens to social deviants with the potential to cause serious harm. Either way, few people who knew the pair suspected their well-planned agenda for April 20, 1999. Ironically, those closest to Harris and Klebold had the least notion of the dire happenings scheduled to occur that spring.

In fact, the Klebolds had already placed a deposit on a college dorm in Arizona, and the Harrises were preparing for their son's postgraduation future. While Harris had been rejected from the U.S. Marine Corps due to the fact that he was taking the antidepressant Luvox, it remains unclear whether he was aware of this as of April 20, 1999. He had been prescribed the drug in conjunction with the court-mandated anger-management therapy that had resulted from his and Klebold's decision to burglarize a van in 1998. A military representative had unsuccessfully attempted to get in touch with Harris, but it is believed that Harris may have already suspected that the corps knew of the prescription and would likely refuse him because of it. In any case, little seemed out of the ordinary to the Harris family as their son got ready for commencement and celebrated his eighteenth birthday in early April.

Obviously, though, Harris's and Klebold's mental states and goals for the future were far from normal. Despite their ability to keep their identities as prospective killers largely closeted, they remained killers all the same. In addition to the gleeful threats of violence they disclosed with great anticipation in their videos, journals, and online compositions, the young men had amassed an impressive weapons collection. Older friends and acquaintances had supplied Harris and Klebold with two shotguns, a rifle, and a semiautomatic pistol starting in late 1998. The teens also had spent several weekends constructing pipe bombs and Molotov cocktails in Harris's garage. Two homemade propane-tank bombs and a bevy of knives rounded out the arsenal. Their weapons cache was to be revealed to the world on "Judgment Day"—a term the pair used to refer to what most of the country would later come to call the Columbine massacre.

Among the personal papers scrutinized by law-enforcement officials after the infamous shooting, authorities discovered that Harris and Klebold had created several maps of their high school, as well as a precise agenda for the timing of April 20, 1999. Harris had even scribbled down the following eerie schedule of events in his planner as he foresaw them occurring on Judgment Day: "5:00: Get up; 6:00: Meet at KS; 7:00: Go to [Klebold's] house; 7:15: [Klebold] leaves to fill propane; I leave to fill gas; 8:30: Meet back at [Klebold's] house; 9:00: Made d. bag set up car; 9:30: Practice gearups; Chill . . .; 10:30: Set up four things; 11:00: Go to school; 11:10: Set up duffel bags; 11:12: Wait near cars, gear up; 11:16: HAHAHA.

The portion of the plan notated "HAHAHA" involved the duffel bags and their deadly contents, which consisted of the propane-tank bombs the boys had constructed. After leaving the bags in the cafeteria, Harris and Klebold planned to wait outside the school and use their other weapons to attack whatever students and teachers fled after the massive explosion that was timed to occur at 11:17 a.m., during Columbine's crowded first-period lunch. The teens calculated that emergency personnel would be delayed due to a distraction they had staged—a few smaller bombs that were planted in a field a short distance from the school and were set to explode at approximately 11:14 a.m.

Much to Harris's and Klebold's disappointment, however, they witnessed no mass exodus of terrified victims as the minutes ticked past 11:17 a.m. Everything else had gone as planned, including their deposit of the duffel bags in the cafeteria earlier in the morning. Brown would later recall the last time he saw Harris and Klebold as they exited the school subsequent to planting the propane-tank bombs inside. Despite the fact that Harris and Brown had experienced a falling out, they had recently patched things up—at least to the point that Harris felt enough empathy to issue the following warning as he and Klebold departed Columbine: "Brooks," Harris cautioned, "I like you now. Get out of here. Go home." Brown, who was preparing to have a cigarette outside the high school, took the words to heart and didn't return that day. As he would shortly discover, it was a decision that saved his life. For as Harris and Klebold eagerly strapped on their arsenal and checked their watches, they began to run out of patience. Something had obviously gone wrong with the propane-tank bombs, so it was time to

The Complex Perspectives of a Student and Friend

Like so many other Columbine students and faculty members, Brown struggled in the aftermath of the massacre. For the then-senior, however, the burden was in some ways doubly hard to shoulder. On the one hand, Harris had previously threatened Brown's life, but the two had since reconciled. In addition, while Brown was friends with both of the killers, he also lost people he knew and cared for as a result of the killers' actions.

As the Columbine alumnus later said of the rampage, "I would go on to lose four friends. Two of them would be the murderers at Columbine. And I'd be ostracized for that fact. It would destroy me. At the time, I couldn't make sense of anything that had happened. I had cut myself off from my family, I had cried in private for hours, and I stayed awake for days on end, simply sitting and watching the news."

improvise. At 11:19 a.m., they did just that. Wearing their black trench coats, they headed back inside to initiate a massacre that would rock Littleton and most of the world.

Beginning of the Bloodshed

Harris and Klebold were so anxious to start their killing spree that they didn't even wait to trudge through the high school's doors before they opened fire. Instead, they climbed a hill near Columbine's west entrance and aimed their guns at students who had gathered outside to eat lunch or to have a cigarette. This initial spray of bullets killed seventeen-year-old Rachel Scott, whom Klebold had known since kindergarten, and injured six others. Fifteen-year-old Daniel Rohrbough was among those who were wounded during the first moments of the Columbine massacre, though he died when Klebold shot him at point-blank range a few minutes later. Klebold then made a quick trip inside the cafeteria to check on the status of the propane-tank bombs that had failed to detonate.

When Klebold returned outside, he and Harris took aim at and injured yet another teen and then proceeded to throw various incendiary devices they were carrying with them in duffel bags all around the exterior of the school. As multitudes of students within Columbine worryingly wondered about the source of the commotion, the first 911 call went out to authorities at 11:23 a.m. Meanwhile, a custodian had notified Jefferson County sheriff's deputy and school resource officer Neil Gardner of the chaos that was unfolding. Eating lunch on the school premises, Gardner—who was armed—hurried to where the pandemonium was reportedly occurring. He first encountered Harris and Klebold as they

Harris and Klebold injured twenty-three people during their shooting spree at Columbine High School.

began to fire into the building, injuring a teacher named Patti Nielson and a student in her company.

Not exactly sure what had been causing all the noise and hysteria near Columbine's west entrance, Nielson had started walking in that direction, intending to tell whoever was behind what she imagined must be a prank or part of an amateur video production to knock it off. She never made it outside, however, as Harris and Klebold shot out the glass on the interior set of doors, wounding both her and the student who had accompanied her. Luckily, she was able to retreat into the high school and instruct anyone she encountered to take cover even before Harris and Klebold had actually entered the building. Teachers and students desperately sought refuge

Taking Delight in Destruction

Apart from the obvious sadness and shock that resulted from the killings themselves, horror at Harris's and Klebold's enthusiasm for the bloodshed baffled and disturbed America. As the teens began the carnage outside their high school, bystanders reported that they were almost giddy with excitement.

"This is what we always wanted to do," one of the gunmen allegedly shouted. "This is awesome!" When later relaying the sequence of the massacre in an official sheriff's report, Jefferson County investigators responded to the killers' attitudes and actions with the following assessment: "While this report establishes a record of the events of April 20, it cannot answer the most fundamental question—WHY? That is, why would two young men in the spring of their lives choose to murder faculty members and classmates? The evidence provides no definitive explanation, and the question continues to haunt us all."

wherever they could, from washroom stalls to utility closets. At that point no one even knew exactly who was shooting or how many perpetrators there were.

Within minutes of arriving on the scene, though, Gardner took aim at Harris and Klebold, the former exchanging gunfire with the officer. Soon afterward, the pair moved inside the high school and progressed along the main north hallway. As they took this first trek through Columbine's interior, they injured one more student and sent others screaming with terror as they pointed their guns at anyone they met, all the while laughing maniacally. Tossing the rest of their homemade pipe bombs left and right, they continued to shoot out windows, causing notable damage to the school's east entrance.

The killers next decided to head west and continued their rampage by proceeding to the library. They took another victim in the process—teacher Dave Sanders. The staffer had been instrumental in evacuating people from the cafeteria when the shooting had started, and sources hypothesize that he was on his way to the library for the same reason. Before Sanders could demonstrate further bravery, however, Harris and Klebold fatally wounded him in the chest. Though a colleague was able to drag him to safety inside a science classroom and students desperately administered first aid, he died less than four hours later.

By 11:29 a.m. several local law-enforcement agents and medical personnel had assembled outside Columbine. If Harris and Klebold were aware of their presence, they remained undeterred. As Harris and Klebold entered the high school's library, they prepared to take revenge on the fifty-six people who had scrambled to that location for safety. During the ensuing massacre, which lasted less than ten minutes, the teenage killers claimed ten additional lives.

Slaughter throughout the Rest of the School

After sustaining wounds when Harris and Klebold shot out the windows at Columbine's western entrance, Nielson had fled to the library, frantically dialing 911 and urging the other staff members and the fifty-two students there to take cover under the tables. The following chilling exchange that transpired between her and the emergency operator reveals but a fraction of the terror that individuals trapped in the library experienced as Harris and Klebold approached.

Nielson: Okay? In the library. And I've got every student in the library — On the floor! You guys, stay on the floor!

Dispatcher: Is there any way you can lock the doors?

Nielson: Um, smoke is coming in from out there and I'm a little — [More shots, louder this time] The gun is right outside the library door, okay? I don't think I'm going to go out there. Okay?

Dispatcher: Okay. You're at Columbine High School?

. . .

One of the shooters: YEAH!!! [Another shot]

Nielson: [whispering] Oh, God. I'm really . . . frightened. [More shots, extremely close] I think he's in the library.

Dispatcher: What's your name, ma'am?

Nielson: [whispering] My name is Patti.

Dispatcher: Patti?
One of the gunman can barely be heard in the background: Everybody get up! Now!

Nielson: [whispering] He's yelling "Everybody get up" right now. [More shots] He's in the library. He's shooting at everybody.

Dispatcher: Okay. I have him in the library shooting at students and . . . the lady in the library, I have on the phone. . . . Okay. Try to keep as many people down as you can.

Sources later claimed that either Harris or Klebold shouted, "All the jocks stand up" and decreed that "anybody with a white hat or a shirt with a sports emblem on it is dead." None of the fifty-six individuals in the library were eager to follow their commands, and they remained in their hiding spots throughout the room. Consequently, Harris and Klebold decided to start shooting at random. Between 11:29

Yellow evidence tags are placed throughout the library where ten students were killed.

a.m. and 11:35 a.m. the pair strolled among the tables, aiming their weapons underneath them and antagonizing their victims before firing. During the library massacre the killers murdered sixteen-year-old Kyle Velasquez, fourteen-year-old Steven Curnow, seventeen-year-old Cassie Bernall, eighteen-year-old Isaiah Shoels, sixteen-year-old Matthew Kechter, eighteen-year-old Lauren Townsend, sixteen-year-old John Tomlin, sixteen-year-old Kelly Fleming, fifteen-year-old Daniel Mauser, and seventeen-year-old Corey DePooter. They injured twelve other teens.

Harris's and Klebold's hatred didn't seem limited to Columbine's jocks. Survivors recall the young men using racial slurs before they shot Shoels, who was African American, as well as reportedly asking some of their victims if they believed in God. Regardless of their exact motivations for murder, however, the horror they instigated in the library was unquestionable—as was their unmistakably cavalier attitude toward killing. Harris and Klebold laughed as they fired their weapons, generally appearing ecstatic during the entire ordeal.

When not shooting at students huddled under tables, they periodically took aim at law-enforcement officials they spotted through the windows. They also continued to detonate their homemade bombs. By 11:35 a.m. Harris and Klebold decided it was time to move on. Roaming through Columbine's hallways once more, they kept up their pattern of shooting randomly and tossing explosives. A video surveillance camera in the cafeteria reveals that they returned there to inspect the propane-tank bombs at about 11:44 a.m. and once more at 11:57 a.m.

Shortly after noon Harris and Klebold returned to the library, which the majority of survivors had fled following the shooters' initial departure mere minutes earlier. Between 12:02 p.m. and 12:05 p.m. the pair positioned themselves at the library's windows and opened fire on police, paramedics, and Special Weapons and Tactics (SWAT) team specialists assembled outside the school. Though law-enforcement officials returned the young men's gunplay, this exchange is not what ultimately killed them.

A Columbine High School surveillance camera captures Harris (left)
and Klebold (right) as they return to the cafeteria to check bombs
placed there earlier.

By approximately 12:08 p.m. Harris had taken his own
life after placing a gun in his mouth and pulling the trigger. Klebold also committed suicide, except he did so via a
single shot to the head. Forty-nine minutes after they had
first started shooting, the Columbine killers themselves lay
lifeless, leaving behind thirteen dead, twenty-three injured,
and a legacy of questions about school violence that continue
to haunt the nation more than a decade later.

Three

Aftermath
of the
Massacre

THE ATMOSPHERE IN LITTLETON AND ACROSS the country immediately after the Columbine massacre was a combination of rage, horror, and confusion. It was a mixture of emotions that would not quickly dissipate in the days, weeks, and even years ahead. How could such atrocities have been committed by perpetrators who were so young, and what could have driven them to their murderous rampage?

These disturbing questions and others like them took over discussions at both nationwide news stations and average American dinner tables on April 20, 1999. And, while everyone from psychology experts to high school students pondered what had occurred that day, SWAT teams and emergency personnel carried out the gruesome and terrifying task of making their way through Columbine High School. As they did so, tearful friends and relatives of Columbine attendees gathered at a nearby elementary school to await further information on the condition of their loved ones. Much to their anxiety, it was not always quick in coming.

When law-enforcement officials entered the building in the early afternoon of April 20, 1999, they still had no idea how many killers were at work or their exact locations in the school. It therefore took them several hours to comb the hallways and classrooms before they confirmed that the perpetrators had committed suicide in the library. In the interim they snuck through Columbine, which was filled with shell casings, shrapnel, remnants of homemade bombs, and waves of smoke that had been dampened by emergency sprinkler systems. Gradually, paramedics and other rescue workers were able to evacuate any students who remained in the school, though many were too terrified even to respond when SWAT teams first called them from their hiding spots. Shortly before 4:00 p.m. authorities discovered Harris's and Klebold's corpses.

Their bodies, along with those of their thirteen victims, could not be removed until the next day, when investigators had had an opportunity to examine and photograph the crime scene. Due to all the explosives that Harris and Klebold had scattered throughout the building, Columbine would not officially be declared safe until April 21, 1999, after a bomb squad had painstakingly searched the premises for evidence of active incendiary devices. After the dead had been identified and retrieved from school grounds, mourners set up memorials that took the form of crosses, flowers, and cards honoring those who had been senselessly slain.

While Columbine students returned to school and attempted to heal and to move ahead, several of the injured and the family members of those who were killed angrily demanded justice in exchange for their pain. They began filing lawsuits against everyone from manufacturers of violent video games such as those Harris and Klebold had

Mourners visit a memorial honoring the victims of the Columbine massacre.

played to the young men's parents to Jefferson County for not placing enough stock in the Browns' complaints about the threats made against their son.

Some of the killers' older acquaintances were eventually prosecuted for providing the pair with weapons they otherwise would not have been able to obtain due to age restrictions, but gun control seemed to be only one factor in the massacre. After all, something deeper must have driven Harris and Klebold to want to use the weapons in question, and that motivating factor seemed more deadly than the ease with which the teens had gotten their hands on the guns.

Even people who were in no way connected to Littleton desperately sought clues to what had triggered the unbelievable slayings. Apart from needing resolution to overcome the grief and shock borne of Harris's and Klebold's actions, Americans were eager for information about the murderers' motivations — perhaps knowing that if such an episode could shake a quiet, middle-class Colorado town to its core, it could likewise happen anywhere.

As then-president Bill Clinton noted of the Columbine massacre during a televised address to the nation on April 22, 1999,

> Even though it is the worst example of school violence we've seen, it is by no means the only one. . . . And I think we have to ask ourselves some pretty hard questions here: What are the responsibilities of students themselves? What are the responsibilities of schools? What are the responsibilities of parents? What is the role of the larger culture here? Is there a sense in which the fact that all of you are exposed to much higher levels of violence through television, through video games, that you can actually figure out how to make bombs on the Internet — does that make a difference? Does it make these kinds of things more likely to happen? What are our responsibilities?

Such were the questions that people would endeavor to answer in the wake of Harris's and Klebold's handiwork.

Bullied into Becoming Killers?

As the world pondered what had spurred the Columbine killing spree, attention inevitably settled on the private and public lives of the perpetrators. Popular opinion was that Harris and Klebold were obviously mentally disturbed, but what—if any—additional factors transformed them from troubled teenagers to cold-blooded murderers? Looking to the young men's families, outsiders speculated about whether there was instability or irregularity within the Harris or Klebold households. According to the videotaped admissions of the killers themselves, however, both had come from loving and secure home environments that—at least from their perspectives—did not in any way contribute to their plans for April 1999.

"My parents are the best . . . parents I have ever known," Harris professed in a video recording he and Klebold made in Harris's car on April 11, 1999. "My dad is great. I wish I was a . . . sociopath so I didn't have any remorse, but I do. This is going to tear them apart. They will never forget it." Speaking directly to his mother and father during taping, he added, "There is nothing you guys could have done to prevent any of this. There is nothing that anyone could have done to prevent this. No one is to blame except me and [Klebold]. Our actions are a two-man war against everyone else."

Despite the fact that in certain instances, Harris and Klebold cleared everyone else of responsibility for their crimes, other video recordings they created clearly contradicted this sentiment. Several referenced how Columbine's athletes and more popular students would suffer the consequences of

Countless Reasons
behind the Killing

Though many theories exist as to what ultimately drove Harris and Klebold to kill, one popular perspective—as explained by Chad Dion Lassiter, president of Black Men at Penn School of Social Work at the University of Pennsylvania in Philadelphia—is that there were several contributing factors. According to this vantage point, the murderers' psychological states, their experiences with social intolerance, and their regular exposure to violence via computer games and movies were all likely to blame in some form or another for the Littleton rampage.

"This is not 'either/or' but 'both/and' with regard to the social cliques and bullying, violent media outlets, use of antidepressants, and [Harris's and Klebold's] various psychological challenges," observed Lassiter during an interview conducted in April 2009. "They all worked in concert as it pertains to the overall development of the Columbine killings."

having ostracized them. After the massacre Klebold's own mother commented on the high school's cliquish atmosphere in relation to her son's actions. "I think he suffered horribly before he died," she observed years after the incident. "For not seeing that, I will never forgive myself." Klebold and her husband went on to reference their son being provoked by the "toxic culture" that pervaded Columbine and that was defined by hero worship of the jocks and the administration's underlying acceptance of various forms of bullying.

Teacher Patti Stevens concurred with their assessment that such attitudes and related forms of harassment too often went unchecked at the high school. "I saw how afraid and scared my [pupils] were," she later explained when speaking of students who were frequent victims of bullying. "I mentioned it at staff meetings. I didn't get any response. They kind of blew me off." From a similar perspective, Betty Shoels, the aunt of the African-American student who was gunned down during the Columbine massacre, relayed how even members of the Trench Coat Mafia were responsible for their share of social harassment. She explained how they often bullied her nephew, along with anyone from a different racial background or anyone they didn't like. When Shoels attempted to speak to school administrators about the situation, she was allegedly told by principal Frank DeAngelis, "We don't have those problems here."

As Stevens, Shoels, and other parents, teachers, and Columbine students came forward after the killings, it became clear that a great percentage of those familiar with the culture of the school agreed with the Klebolds' belief that intimidation and harassment played a role in day-to-day life there. Consequently, the public began to wonder if the violence of April 20, 1999, might have been avoided if bullying and the social stigmatization that accompanies it had been dealt with more aggressively by administrators. If Harris and Klebold had not been victims of harassment initiated by the athletes, and if, in turn, they and other members of the Trench Coat Mafia had not been permitted to bully minorities such as Shoels, would they have regarded their fellow students with less hatred and greater respect? For his part, DeAngelis denied that any form of social intimidation possibly connected to the case was ever brought to his attention.

"If it was occurring," the principal asserted, "it was not being reported." DeAngelis further went on to question the accuracy of portraying Harris and Klebold as victimized targets. "If [Klebold] was alienated, why did he show up at the prom?" he questioned. "Why did [Harris] show up at after prom?" In fact, both young men had made appearances at the school prom only days before, yet Devon Adams, a Columbine attendee and acquaintance of the pair, argued that this did not mean they were not bullied and harassed. "They were teased constantly," she recalled. "[They were] called faggots, psychos, and freaks. And not just by jocks. There were students who worked in the drama department who were mean to them. By no means does it excuse it, but I think they felt really alone and alienated, [and] they didn't know who to turn to." Regardless of conflicting perspectives on the level of bullying at Columbine and the degree of tolerance administrators demonstrated toward it, most of the public agreed with Adams's emphasis that no amount of social ostracizing in the high school's halls justified Harris's and Klebold's actions.

Americans began to look beyond what transpired on a day-to-day basis within Columbine and started to seek outside factors that may have played a role in the April 1999 killings. One question they asked themselves was if violence in the media—a widely accepted element in U.S. culture—was to blame for violence within the country's schools.

From Computer Games to Actual Carnage

In the wake of a massacre that left fifteen people dead, nearly two dozen injured, and a school in shambles, some people found it hard to imagine that two teenagers' obsession with sitting at a computer and clicking a mouse could correlate with such widespread destruction. Yet Harris's and Klebold's friends and family were aware that both young men were deeply fascinated by the computer game *Doom*, which allows players to assume the role of first-person shooters in an online world filled with graphic violence. The program is, in fact, licensed by the U.S. military to help train soldiers for combat.

But was Harris's and Klebold's fascination enough to prompt them to become killers? From the perspective of psychologists Craig Anderson and Karen Dill, the answer is yes. They conducted a study whose results were published in 2000. Noting that Harris actually created his own online version of *Doom* that featured two shooters and victims who lacked the capacity to fight back, the researchers quoted an investigator who had worked on the Columbine case and who believed that the boys were "playing out their game in God mode." Anderson and Dill added, "Entertainment media affects our lives. What behavior children and adults consider appropriate comes, in part, from the lessons we learn from television and the movies. There are good theoretical reasons to expect that violent video games will have similar and possibly larger effects on aggression."

Nor was computerized entertainment the only medium that fell under scrutiny in connection to the Columbine massacre. Harris and Klebold had also been avid fans of violent movies such as *Natural Born Killers*, which highlights the actions of two mass murderers, and *The Basketball Diaries*, which depicts the protagonist fantasizing about assaulting his classmates.

The Basketball Diaries, a film depicting a classroom shooting, was one of Harris's and Klebold's favorites.

Even before April 20, 1999, *Natural Born Killers* had been accused of sparking a series of crimes similar to the atrocities committed on-screen. After the slaughter at Columbine the public once again had occasion to wonder if such movies and games like *Doom* were setting the stage for episodes of extreme violence. Since teenagers were absorbing the media messages in question, it made sense that any resulting outbursts of aggression were likely to take place in an environment where young people spend a great deal of their time—school.

This connection appeared reasonable to Harris's and Klebold's victims and their familes. Consequently, these men and women filed a lawsuit against twenty-five computer-game manufacturers, including such big-name companies as Sony America, AOL/TimeWarner, ID Software, Atari, Sega of America, Virgin Interactive Media, Activision, Polygram Film Entertainment Distribution, New Line Cinema, GT Interactive Software, and Nintendo. The suit alleged that "Absent the combination of extremely violent video games and these boys' incredibly deep involvement, use of, and addiction to these games and the boys' basic personalities, these murders and this massacre would not have occurred."

Put another way, plaintiffs' lawyers acknowledged that Harris and Klebold were obviously mentally disturbed to begin with but argued that the violent nature of *Doom* had exacerbated their psychological issues until the young men hit a breaking point. A federal judge disagreed in March 2002 and dismissed the case. From the perspective of U.S. district judge Lewis Babcock, the accused manufacturers could not possibly have predicted that their product would elicit the bloodshed that Harris and Klebold caused. He further added that censoring the media to potentially prevent violence in schools or anywhere else would pose a serious threat to Americans' freedom of speech.

"Setting aside any personal distaste," Babcock noted, "it is [apparent] that there is social utility in expressive and imaginative forms of entertainment, even if they contain violence." Those individuals who agreed with the judge's opinions referenced all the average people who routinely watch gory movies or play violent video games without ever committing any type of crime or serious act of aggression. Yet, according to psychology professor Douglas Gentile at Iowa State University in Ames, such a perspective is simply too black and white. "We all know that we've watched lots of media violence and [have] never gone on a shooting rampage," Gentile commented in 2007, "but that is not where we should look for the effects. The effects are more subtle. In order to do something seriously violent, one must have multiple risk factors for aggression — media violence is only one risk factor, and it's not the largest one. It's also not the smallest."

This perspective returned discussion of the Columbine massacre to the killers' own personalities. Whether media violence or school cliques and bullying had pushed Harris and Klebold over the edge, the pair clearly had been disturbed enough to begin with that they became psychologically imbalanced. Even Harris's use of antidepressants was analyzed for its possible role in the murders. But as a troubled country considered and debated precisely what drove the teens to destruction, Americans also started sharing different perspectives on how the Columbine massacre could be used to prevent similar incidents of school violence.

Vantage Points on a Controversial Computer Game

In light of the popular perspective that violence in the media was at least partially to blame for Harris's and Klebold's shooting spree, it was no great surprise that the majority of survivors and families and friends of the Columbine victims were appalled by *Super Columbine Massacre RPG!* The computer game, which has been available online since 2005, essentially allows players to reenact the April 1999 rampage from the vantage point of the killers.

"I've been living with Columbine for seven years," noted Brown in 2006. "This game is just deplorable. It shouldn't surprise me, living in the kind of world we're living in, but it does surprise me." Yet from the perspective of Danny Ledonne, the game's creator, Super Columbine Massacre RPG! was never intended to celebrate school violence or to undermine its impact. "I'm not advocating shooting up your school," he explained, "and I don't know how many times I can say that and no one will listen. This game does not glorify school shootings. If you make it far enough in the game, you see very graphic photos of Eric and Dylan lying dead. I can't think of a more effective way to confront their actions and the consequences those actions had."

Four

Using the Past to Prevent Repetition

IF ANYTHING POSITIVE RESULTED FROM the bloodshed of April 20, 1999, it was that it forced the public to become more aware of school violence and more proactive in preventing it. DeAngelis, the principal of Columbine both now and at the time of the shootings, summed up the impact that incident had on people across the nation. As he explained, men and women who previously thought themselves safe, secure, and far from the reach of the Eric Harrises and Dylan Klebolds of the world suddenly had to reevaluate their proximity to potential school violence.

"Columbine served as a wakeup call," observed DeAngelis on April 13, 2009—mere days away from the tenth anniversary of the killings. "No one can ever say, 'It could never happen here.'" Naturally, as people all over the country began to realize that the events that transpired at Columbine could repeat themselves closer to home, they also started to consider how the massacre in Littleton could have been prevented.

This process of reflection and the evaluation of the situation in hindsight could not resurrect Harris's and Klebold's thirteen victims or erase the trauma experienced by the students and teachers who survived their rampage. Yet the individuals who analyzed the Columbine massacre reasoned that the various perspectives they brought to the table might help people from parents and school administrators to expert psychologists and law-enforcement agents stop similar episodes of school violence.

Gauging the Role of Gun Control

One age-old debate awakened by the killings surrounded gun control. After the massacre, investigators determined that Harris's and Klebold's then–eighteen-year-old friend Robyn Anderson had purchased weapons for the boys at a gun show in December 1998. In addition, law-enforcement officials discovered that Mark Manes—one of the perpetrators' coworkers at Blackjack—had sold them firearms in early 1999. Manes was eventually given a prison sentence for his role in the tragedy, as was another older acquaintance, Philip Duran, who had acted as a middleman in the transaction. Though authorities declared that Anderson had not committed a crime when she bought the guns in late 1998, as she reportedly believed they would be used either for hunting or as collectors' items, she nonetheless expressed deep regret about any part she unwittingly played in the shootings:

> When Eric and Dylan had gone [to the
> gun show] . . . a dealer told them that they
> needed to bring someone back who was
> eighteen. They were both seventeen at
> the time. This was a private dealer—not
> a licensed dealer. While we were walking

around, Eric and Dylan kept asking sellers
if they were private or licensed. They
wanted to buy their guns from someone
who was private—and not licensed—
because there would be no paperwork or
background check. . . . They [eventually]
bought guns from three sellers. They were
all private. They paid cash. There was no
receipt. I was not asked any questions at
all. There was no background check. All
I had to do was show my driver's license
to prove that I was eighteen. . . . I wish a
law requiring background checks had been
in effect at the time. I don't know if Eric
and Dylan would have been able to get
guns from another source, but I would not
have helped them. It was too easy. I wish
it had been more difficult. I wouldn't have
helped them buy the guns if I had faced a
background check.

As many Americans learned in the aftermath of the Columbine tragedy, gun-control legislation varies from state to state and from county to county, though some standard federal laws such as the following do apply, especially in conjunction with age restrictions: "A person must be twenty-one years of age to purchase a handgun or handgun ammunition and eighteen years of age to buy a rifle or shotgun or ammunition from a retail firearm dealer. . . . A person under age eighteen may not possess a handgun or handgun ammunition, and it is illegal for a person to provide a handgun or handgun ammunition to a person under age eighteen, except for target shooting, hunting, or certain other exempted purposes."

As several proponents of stricter gun-control measures pointed out, these legalities often become watered down and lose their value in the face of state and local ordinances that offer exceptions to otherwise hard-and-fast rules. For example, Colorado law currently stipulates that people younger than eighteen can be in possession of a handgun for purposes related to hunting or target practice. Advocates of more rigid gun control argued that the bloodshed of April 20, 1999, might never have come to pass if all dealers at gun shows—and not just those with licenses—had been forced to conduct background checks. And, from the perspective of Columbine survivors such as Nielson, more rigorous gun restrictions mandated by the federal government would likely have hindered Harris and Klebold and could help prevent similar incidents from taking place.

Thousands of protesters rally for stricter gun control at the capitol in Denver on May 1, 1999.

"I've not become an activist, and I certainly won't run for Congress," Nielson said at a news conference she gave during her lobbying efforts in Washington, D.C., in 2000. "I want to be an art teacher, a mom, and a wife. But I'm here today because I'm wondering: 'Why hasn't Congress done anything to prevent what happened at Columbine from happening again?'. . . . The shocking thing is that [Harris and Klebold] got those guns so easily from a gun show."

Not everyone analyzing the prevention of school violence within the framework of Columbine agreed with Nielson's perspective. Members of the National Rifle Association (NRA) and other opponents of tougher gun-control laws argued that passing stricter legislation threatens Americans' Second Amendment right—the right to bear arms. They further objected to the idea that such measures would have stopped the massacre in Littleton from occurring. "No gun show crackdown would have prevented Columbine," observed Dave Kopel, author of *The Truth About Gun Shows*:

> The older of the two killers could have bought his guns in a store legally, since he turned eighteen before the Columbine attack. Indeed, in a videotape made before the killings, the murderers said that if they had not obtained their guns the way they did, they would have found other ways. There is no reason to disbelieve them on this point. . . . Whatever the other merits of proposals to impose special restrictions on gun shows, these would not have prevented Columbine, and it is chillingly cynical for their proponents to use Columbine as a pretext.

Ironic Evidence of the Need for Firearms?

From the perspective of Janalee Tobias, the president and founder of Women Against Gun Control (WAGC), which is based out of South Jordan, Utah, the Columbine killings served as evidence that America should *not* create more rigorous gun-control laws. According to Tobias, the massacre was proof that U.S. citizens live in a violent society in which an unrestricted right to bear arms is a necessity.

"Columbine shattered any remaining hopes of schools being the safest place in the world," she noted on the tenth anniversary of the slayings. "School shootings and mass public shootings have dramatically increased. . . . We've sadly come to the realization that any one of us could become a victim of violent crime anytime, anywhere. I believe that people with differing views on gun control can work together to find solutions to stop the violence. In the meantime, this mom will cling to her guns and religion for her protection."

As proponents of stricter gun control would soon discover, their efforts remained at the forefront of federal, state, and local legislative affairs immediately following Columbine but largely fell by the wayside as time elapsed. While lawmakers initially considered a slew of proposed bills that addressed everything from mandatory child safety locks on new handguns to requirements for more extensive background checks at gun shows, the majority of these measures eventually perished amidst congressional debates. Nonetheless, differing perspectives on the link between gun control and student aggression have continued to resurface and intensify on the heels of every tragedy similar to the Columbine massacre—which sadly was not the last act of school violence to plague the nation.

Social Awareness and School Safety

While the public wondered if the events of April 20, 1999, might have been avoided had Harris and Klebold not been able to lay their hands on deadly weapons so easily, Americans were also forced to examine broader and more complex issue of social awareness. Specifically, people across the nation began to speculate whether there are accurate ways to determine if someone is likely to perpetrate school violence. Those connected with Columbine especially analyzed this issue and debated whether measures ranging from more aggressively addressing overt threats to student profiling could have prevented the tragedy.

For example, several Littleton residents, including Brown's parents, were adamant that some of the young men's behavior that was brought to the attention of authorities prior to the shootings should have been taken as legitimate warning signs of their potential for violence. Controversy continues to swirl more than a decade later regarding how much further Jefferson County authorities should have pushed to search Harris's home after the Browns made police aware of his Web page, which contained numerous threats and even information about his handcrafted bomb collection. Shortly after the murders, local investigators admitted, "We got some information about some kids who didn't get along, [and] some information . . . was provided on a Web page that we could not verify." At the same time, however, they excused their failure to pursue the matter by insisting, "Kids in virtually every high school in the country at times don't get along."

Similar speculation arose over how seriously Columbine High School staff and Klebold's own parents should have taken hints about the bloodshed to come that were contained in a graphic essay he composed for an English class two months before the massacre. His story glorifies a killer who wears a black trench coat and brutally slaughters several victims outside a bar. Though Klebold's teacher gave him complimentary feedback such as "great details" and "quite an ending," she also was disturbed enough about the essay to contact his family. In turn, they allegedly responded to her concerns with nonchalant comments about "trying to understand kids these days."

Parents and educators must walk a fine line between brushing off the sometimes eccentric behavior of "kids these days" and seriously evaluating the warning signs of aggressive tendencies. Some experts argued that not even the slightest hint of impending violence can be treated lightly within a school setting, even if the individual behind it writes

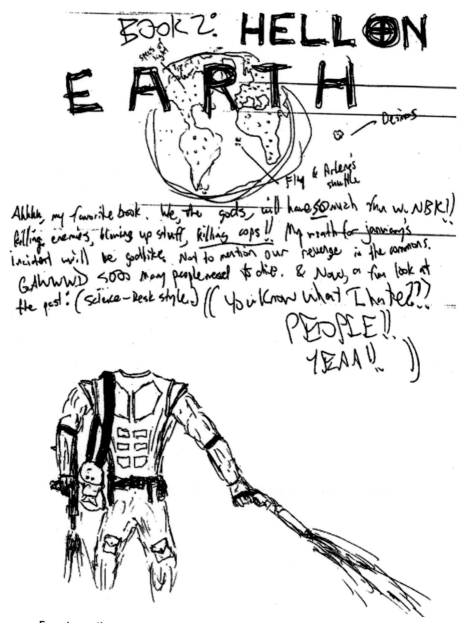

BOOK 2: HELL ON EARTH

Ahhhh, my favorite book. We, the gods, will have so much fun w. NBK!)
killing enemies, blowing up stuff, killing cops! My wrath for January's
incident will be godlike. Not to mention our revenge in the commons.
GAHWWD sooo many people need to die. & Now, a fun look at
the past! (science-Desk style.) ((You know what I hate??!
PEOPLE!!
YEAA!!))

Experts continue to analyze documents that once belonged to Harris and
Klebold for clues related to if and how the Columbine massacre could have
been prevented.

off his or her words or actions as a joke or an odd expression of creativity. According to Federal Bureau of Investigation (FBI) special agent Harry Trombitas, it is crucial to take a closer look at any possible sign that a student has the capability to lash out at those around him.

"You cannot afford to not follow up on *any* kind of threat," he explained in an article on school violence published by the *Columbus Dispatch* in 2008. "The more specific a threat is, the more seriously it needs to be addressed." Though few people contested Trombitas's perspective within the framework of Columbine, some did caution that not every student who makes a threat should be classified as violent. In the summer of 1999 the FBI's National Center for the Analysis of Violent Crime organized a conference to address school shootings. In conjunction with feedback from the U.S. Secret Service and the U.S. Department of Education, attendees concluded that each threat needs to be assessed individually, with experts at the meeting noting, "All threats are not created equal."

Moreover, several of the men and women at the conference observed the importance of distinguishing between students who make actual threats and those who simply appear to have the stereotypical characteristics of a school shooter, as exemplified by Harris and Klebold. Even the FBI's own profiling experts warned "against the use of student profiling to identify potential school shooters." Psychologists are sometimes able to link certain common features shared by the perpetrators of school massacres, including bouts of depression or suicidal thoughts, feelings of social victimization that often result from bullying, and an attraction to violently graphic video games. That acknowledged, however, FBI agents also emphasized how impractical it would be to

Averting School Violence with the ARMS System

Is there an exact science to evaluating threats of school violence? Several academic institutions cooperate with law-enforcement agencies in utilizing a system based on assessment, referral, monitoring, and support (ARMS). When a threat is made, assessment teams consisting of both on-site faculty members and local authorities work together to determine whether a student's behavior might result in harm to himself or other people. They typically use eleven questions developed by the U.S. Department of Education to evaluate the specific situation, including queries such as "Are other people concerned about the student's potential for violence?" and "What circumstances might affect the likelihood of an attack?"

Depending on the outcome of the assessment, the author of the threat may be referred for social or psychological services, such as counseling. A behavioral support plan and a monitoring strategy might also be implemented by faculty. These tactics help ensure that the student in question doesn't slip through the cracks. In addition, they provide specific ways for staff to give an individual the attention and assistance he needs to handle situations that may have prompted the threat in the first place.

The ARMS system is also effective in uncovering and addressing instances of bullying and mental crises that might otherwise go unnoticed in a classroom or campus setting. The idea is not to treat just one particular threat but to understand and work with young people to help them resolve the underlying issues that caused them to con- template school violence.

use these traits exclusively to single out possible killers in an effort to prevent school violence. After all, though some bullied outcasts such as Harris and Klebold ultimately do commit murder, not every student who is teased or on the fringes of the teenage social scene goes on to do the same. Columbine attendees such as Brown exemplified this fact. Brown's own father described his son and the killers as outcasts and kids who didn't fit in, but only two of the three young men went on to take innocent lives.

From the perspective of Allan Garcia, a sergeant with the police department in Middletown, Rhode Island, and a nationally recognized instructor in the prevention of school violence, social awareness is key when it comes to avoiding bloodshed similar to that which occurred in Littleton, but there is no set of hard-and-fast guidelines to follow. In his opinion, there is no single profile that is matched by every potential school shooter, and not every threat—though each deserves to be taken seriously—is seriously intended by the student behind it. "Not every loner who is wearing black is a killer," explained Garcia when interviewed several years after Columbine. "And not every killer is a loner wearing black. You can't really tell. There's no one thing that links the profiles of these people. If you look at them, all you'll usually see is that they're little kids."

With such varying perspectives on what might have prevented the Columbine massacre and what could stop further incidents of school violence from occurring, it's easy to comprehend how administrators, authorities, and students themselves felt—and continue to feel—both frustrated and afraid in the wake of April 20, 1999. Garcia addressed such emotions by adding that, as critical as prevention is to the process of dealing with shootings like the one in Littleton, so is knowing how to respond when they actually occur. For as the world would painfully discover post-Columbine, even the most thoughtful debates and discussions dedicated to avoiding school violence would not make Harris's and Klebold's actions an isolated incident.

Five

The Iconic Shooting

"YOU HAVE VANDALIZED MY HEART, raped my soul, and torched my conscience. . . . You had a hundred billion chances and ways to have avoided today. But you decided to spill my blood. . . . This is it. This is where it all ends. End of the road. What a life it was. Some life." So spoke Seung-Hui Cho, the twenty-three-year-old English major at Virginia Polytechnic Institute and State University in Blacksburg, Virginia, who killed thirty-two people during a school massacre he orchestrated on April 16, 2007. Apart from becoming recognized as the deadliest peacetime shooting carried out by a single gunman in U.S. history, the disturbed college senior's bloody rampage also returned the public's attention to the Columbine killings, which had taken place almost exactly eight years before.

Referencing "martyrs like Eric and Dylan" in a multimedia manifesto he created prior to slaying his victims and ultimately committing suicide, Cho appeared to revere the Littleton perpetrators. Like them, he undeniably fostered a deep resentment toward other students, by whom he felt victimized. In addition, he was also reportedly bullied while at Virginia Tech and carefully planned his murders well in advance, just as Harris and Klebold had. Upon evaluating such connections, several experts expressed the chilling opinion that not every link between the Columbine killers and Cho was random. From their perspective the events of April 20, 1999, had almost set standards that future perpetrators of school violence hoped to meet.

Seung-Hui Cho sent this photo of himself as part of a multimedia manifesto he delivered to the National Broadcasting Company shortly before going on a killing spree at Virginia Polytechnic University in Blacksburg, Virginia.

An Unwelcome Iconic Status

To many Columbine survivors the public's perception of the Littleton massacre as the iconic act of school violence has a definite downside. Specifically, Patrick Ireland—a student who escaped the carnage by dropping from a second-story library window—told reporters in 2009 that he believes that status still hurts the school. He emphasized that Columbine's past and present attendees and faculty members have struggled to move beyond the incident and have subsequently accomplished a great deal. Those achievements are overshadowed by the events of April 20, 1999, and their standing as a benchmark of classroom violence.

"I hate it when people say, 'Oh, another Columbine-like [tragedy] or Columbine-esque tragedy,'" said Ireland. "Columbine is a school. The shooting was an event that happened [there], and a lot of people have been able to overcome so many things from that."

"[Columbine is] the iconic shooting," observed Katherine S. Newman, a professor of sociology and public affairs at Princeton University, during an interview conducted in preparation for the tenth anniversary of the Littleton massacre. "It defined the social category of a rampage school shooting. . . . Subsequent shooters who have been fueled by a kind of competitive urge cite Columbine first, foremost, and always." By following in the footsteps of Harris and Klebold, killers such as Cho and others continue to force Americans to reevaluate their perspectives on the nation's epidemic of school violence.

Looking for Answers
After Virginia Tech

As was the case after Columbine, the public frantically searched for answers to explain a senseless crime in the wake of the Virginia Tech shootings. For those individuals connected to the 1999 slaying, Cho's actions served as a grim reminder of their unresolved questions and pain. They not only recalled the trauma of losing friends, relatives, and acquaintances, but also experienced the need to reevaluate the Littleton massacre and subsequent school shootings in an effort to prevent similar episodes of violence.

"Immediately, my thoughts went back to April 20, 1999, and vivid memories," admitted DeAngelis in speaking of his initial reactions to the Virginia Tech killings. "It retraumatizes you." Littleton resident Dawn Anna, who lost her daughter Lauren Townsend during Harris's and Klebold's rampage, echoed DeAngelis's sentiments. "I felt like I was looking at

Lauren's murderer," the grief-stricken mother said of footage released of Cho and the chaos he caused at Virginia Tech. "It's as if someone has been cruelly replaying April 20." Yet for some, anger was intermingled with a revival of deep-rooted sorrow, especially given that earlier that month, Judge Babcock made the decision to seal testimony given by Harris's and Klebold's parents for a period of twenty years.

As those individuals touched by the Virginia Tech tragedy mourned and survivors of the Columbine slaughter prepared to observe its eighth anniversary, many Americans couldn't help but voice the perspective that Judge Babcock's decision was a mistake. From their vantage point the known similarities between Harris and Klebold and Cho were too striking to be ignored. Both incidents featured killers who dropped hints of their violent intentions and left written and videotaped explanations of their behavior. In addition, each young man perceived murder as a means to avenge injustices that he believed had been committed by fellow students. Though Cho was allegedly far more of a loner than Harris or Klebold, sources indicate that all three were bullied, and many experts assert that all three spent a great deal of time strategizing an attack in response.

So why, several members of the public wondered, would Babcock not reveal evidence that might further contribute to the profile of a school shooter? With so many links between Columbine and Virginia Tech, it seemed reasonable to assume that any clue that added to the portrait of a perpetrator of classroom violence would be invaluable as a preventive tool. Cho's rampage and its similarities to Harris's and Klebold's murders served as proof to many people that just such information was the key to saving countless lives in the future.

"I don't think you can stop every crazy person," explained Don Fleming, father of another Columbine victim. "But some of the things Babcock locked up show what these crazy kids did. It's no use to anybody if it is locked up. If society knew, it could possibly prevent future shootings. We're finding out that everything that [Cho] did is similar to what Klebold and Harris did." Sociologist Katherine S. Newman reiterated Fleming's opinions and added her own commentary about the danger of concealing data related to Columbine: "A twenty-year lag deprives the rest of the country of what might be valuable insight," she said during a 2007 interview. "Indeed, having done a lot of research with the families of victims, they are left with a big hole in the middle not only by the loss of their children but [also] by the unanswered 'why' questions."

From the perspective of Babcock and his supporters, too much information can sometimes be a bad thing — especially where violence in the classroom is concerned. Though the judge declined to comment officially, he ruled that his decision to conceal the testimony of the Harris and Klebold families was based both on a desire to respect their privacy and on an attempt to prevent copycat killers from manipulating additional resources to repeat the Columbine rampage.

Suggesting a compromise that would address such concerns, Del Elliott, director of the University of Colorado's Center for the Study and Prevention of Violence (CSPV) in

Varying Perspectives on Getting inside the Mind of a Killer

Following the Virginia Tech massacre, friends and family members of the victims were also forced to tackle the issue of how much information is too much when evaluating school shootings. After NBC aired portions of videotaped messages, pictures, and writings that Cho had mailed to the network shortly before he began his rampage, some people felt that the material was too disturbing to be broadcast. Others protested that even though the killer was dead, NBC was essentially providing him with the opportunity to explain his behavior and possibly even to inspire other deranged individuals who were liable to instigate school violence.

"I want this period of time, at least for now, to focus on my daughter, her achievements and all the other kids," said Tony Sherman, father of a Columbine victim, on *The Oprah Winfrey Show* in April 2007 in reaction to NBC's decision. "I just don't want to focus on this . . . one sick individual that did this." Heralding from a different perspective, however, NBC News president Steve Capus defended his network's actions. "This is as close as we'll ever come to being in the mind of a killer," he explained. "Sometimes good journalism is bad public relations. These are very difficult decisions. Remember, this was days after the incident. The largest question out there was 'Why?'"

Boulder, Colorado, proposed that the information in question be made available only to certain parties for scholarly purposes. Though Babcock never altered his ruling, Elliott argued that such data could be put to use in identifying the motives and underlying mental factors behind incidents like Columbine and Virginia Tech. At the same time, however, he acknowledged that it would not be safe for the public to have unlimited access to the testimony. "We know there have been copycat events going on," Elliott observed, "attempts to outdo Columbine. Fortunately, most of them have been thwarted. But there are a lot of kids who obsess about what happened at Columbine. The potential for copycats is real."

Luckily, not every copycat killer who looks to the Littleton massacre has proven successful in his endeavors. And despite the varying perspectives on how the public's ability to analyze *all* the information connected to Columbine could prevent future rampages, it is indisputable that average Americans are at least more aware of school violence since April 20, 1999. As students at Green Bay East High School in Green Bay, Wisconsin, discovered in September 2006, that awareness and the proactive communities it creates can ultimately save lives.

A Columbine Waiting to Happen

For seventeen-year-old William Cornell and Shawn Sturtz, Harris and Klebold were far from deranged killers. In fact, the pair of young men, who attended Green Bay East, regarded the Littleton teens as heroes to be revered and as icons whose actions deserved to be repeated. Consequently,

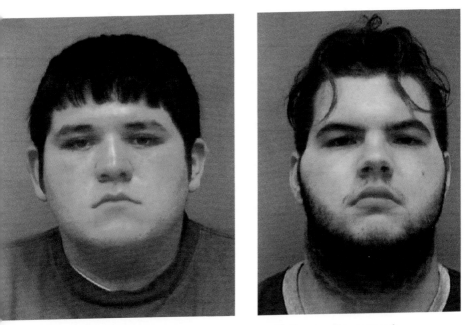

Cornell (left) and Sturtz (right) were obsessed with the shooting spree at Columbine and plotted one of their own at their high school in Green Bay, Wisconsin, in 2006.

Cornell and Sturtz, whom sources later described as being obsessed with the Columbine massacre and deeply resentful of their school and classmates, began planning a shooting spree of their own. They went so far as to prepare suicide notes that they intended to be read after their deaths, which they projected would result from police gunfire during their rampage at Green Bay East.

They were joined in their strategizing sessions by a slightly older teenage acquaintance named Bradley Netwal. Over time the trio managed to acquire an intimidating weapons cache that included napalm, nine rifles and shotguns, a handgun, about twenty handmade explosive devices, camouflage attire, gas masks, two-way radios, and countless rounds of ammunition. In addition, police later discovered Cornell had in his possession a black trench coat and a copy of a book titled *Bully: A True Story of High School Revenge*.

Though no specific date had been set for what may have become the Green Bay East massacre—and despite the fact that each of the three perpetrators periodically removed himself from and later rejoined the plot—the threat they posed was real and ongoing. Luckily for their fellow students, however, Sturtz made a mistake in September 2006 when he revealed their plans to seventeen-year-old friend and classmate Matt Atkinson. Lamenting his recent breakup with a young woman and revealing suicidal thoughts, Sturtz also confessed that he intended to "shoot the place up."

Knowing that the place he was referring to was Green Bay East, Atkinson probed his acquaintance for more information. Sturtz subsequently informed him of the agenda he shared with Cornell and Netwal. "Well, what do you mean, like Columbine?" Atkinson asked in response to the chilling admission. "Well, yeah, exactly," Sturtz is said to have replied. Thanks to Atkinson, though, his friend's plan for murder and mayhem would be foiled. Rattled by what he had heard, Atkinson reported the conversation to an associate principal on September 14, 2006, and both Cornell and Sturtz were arrested within hours. Netwal was taken into custody the following day. The first two young men were accused of conspiracy to commit first-degree intentional homicide and were sentenced to six and three years in prison, respectively. After participating in a plea bargain, Netwal's charge was reduced to conspiracy to commit damages with explosives, and his time behind bars was limited to eighteen months.

"This was a Columbine waiting to happen," observed Brown County district attorney John Zakowski. Green Bay police chief Craig Van Schyndle added, "From statements that we heard, it gave us great concern that, yes, it was in the very near future something was going to take place." From Atkinson's perspective, however, whether or not Sturtz's confession was rooted in truth, he had little choice but to speak up, especially in light of what had transpired in Littleton seven years before.

"I decided it was my duty to inform the authorities," he explained. "If it wasn't true, and I told the authorities, at least [Cornell and Sturtz] would get the help they needed. If I didn't [tell], and they were serious, I couldn't live with all that on my conscience." Yet despite the public's increased awareness of school violence post-Columbine, not everyone at Green Bay East initially shared Atkinson's vantage point. Investigators believed that additional students had heard Cornell and Sturtz speaking of their intended attack but made the choice not to alert law enforcement or school officials. One young woman in whom Cornell had expressed romantic interest even admitted that he had told her he wanted to instigate a shooting rampage in a school or library so that police would ultimately be forced to take his life. "I believe there probably were other people who knew about it," remarked Green Bay detective Tom Molitor. "It was very good luck that [Atkinson] came forward."

According to a report issued by the U.S. Secret Service and the U.S. Department of Education in May 2008, not enough students do come forward for a variety of reasons. Despite Columbine, many of the interviewees expressed a perspective similar to that of one young adult who confessed that it was "hard to believe [a school shooting] could happen" in his own community. Sadly, the source in question later came to regret his point of view after he did nothing when a friend bragged to him about his plans for a killing spree. The threat ultimately resulted in school violence and the death of several classmates.

According to the report, other students did not approach authorities in such instances because they believed their peers were only joking around or displaying bravado. An alternate perspective government researchers encountered amongst young people was rooted in their assumption that authority figures were already aware of the potential problems posed by their troubled classmates and that teachers and administrative officials "had everything under control." Luckily, regardless of students' attitudes about why it was best not to voice their concerns about threats of school violence, a fraction of those interviewed referenced Columbine and how it impacted their decision to act just as Atkinson had at Green Bay East. "If not for Columbine, I might have thought twice about coming forward," one source emphasized, "but I couldn't be one of those who sat by."

In the decade since Harris and Klebold wreaked havoc on their Littleton high school, many Americans have also found it hard to sit by, saying and doing nothing to prevent future violence from erupting in the classroom. Their research into promoting school safety while practicing social tolerance is part of what helps people across the nation remember and learn from Columbine more than ten years later.

Six

A Decade after the Destruction

MORE THAN A DECADE AFTER SHOTS RANG OUT at Columbine, most experts have come to the conclusion that there is no single solution to ending school violence. As incidents such as the Virginia Tech massacre prove, there is no guarantee that the other Eric Harrises and Dylan Klebolds of the world won't attempt to orchestrate violence in America's classrooms. That said, average citizens, school administrators, and authorities are doing whatever they can to educate themselves about school violence to help stop it from occurring.

These individuals bring different perspectives to the table about what can and should be done. Many believe that one of the best ways to prevent violence is increasing school security. Video cameras, metal detectors, security lights, and controlling access to school buildings are among the physical precautions several institutions have put in place post-Columbine. A heightened police presence, backpack checks, and lockdown drills are additional measures educational facilities have begun to employ. While some critics argue that these efforts have transformed America's schools into prisons, proponents respond that the inability to use student profiling to call out prospective killers make the tactics a necessity.

Security supervisors stand guard as students walk through metal detectors in a Chicago, Illinois, high school.

"People think that a school shooter has a certain look to them," observed Gary Rose, director of security for the Brockport School District in Brockport, New York, in April 2009. "Well, it could be anybody." While acknowledging that fact, a large percentage of Americans still feel that placing so great an emphasis on the physical technology behind violence prevention within schools is a costly and somewhat reactionary response to episodes like Columbine.

Determining Progress a Decade Later

As Americans prepared for the tenth anniversary of the Columbine slayings, questions arose about how far the nation had actually come in terms of eliminating school violence. According to a 2007 report from the National Center for Education Statistics (NCES) and the Bureau of Justice Statistics (BJS), "there [had] been about half as many deaths per year since Columbine as in the seven school years before the tragedy." That said, a study conducted by Community Matters titled "The Report Card on School Violence-Prevention" only gave the country a grade of D+.

The nonprofit's scoring system was "based on a careful review of existing school violence and climate data and Community Matters' experience working with hundreds of schools nationwide as part of its Safe School Ambassadors program." After disclosing the less-than-impressive grade in 2009, Phillips encouraged the public to view the D+ as a challenge for the future. "The report card is not an indictment of any individual school system, policy, or leadership team," he explained. "Rather, it is a call to action for all of us to work together to find more effective solutions."

"Immediately after any of these incidents, I think there's the immediate rush for more security," said William Modzeleski, an official with the U.S. Department of Education, during an interview conducted in anticipation of the tenth anniversary of the killings. "That's what I would call the knee-jerk reaction to any type of these events: 'We need more cops; we need more metal detectors; we need more cameras.' After that settles in, I think people come to their senses and say, 'Hey, if we're going to keep our kids safe in schools, we need more than that.'"

Rick Phillips, executive director of a nonprofit violence-prevention organization called Community Matters, expressed similar sentiments. "You can check the guns at the door with metal detectors, but you can't check the kids at the door," he explained. "If you want to stop the violence, don't just try to keep the guns out of school. Change the environment so a student doesn't want to bring a gun to school." This attitude has convinced many students and educators that preventing another Columbine is not so much a matter of installing metal detectors and cameras as it is about encouraging social awareness and tolerance.

Altering the Atmosphere

School officials who feel that stopping guns and bombs from entering the building is only part of the answer to ending school violence believe it's even more important to create an atmosphere that fosters open communication and acceptance. Since the Columbine massacre, many government agencies and educational institutions have set up special hotlines and message stations that anonymous tipsters can use to phone in or e-mail information regarding threats of a potential rampage. For example, the State of Colorado established a call center known as Safe2Tell that, in the past four and a half years, has helped prevent twenty-eight planned school attacks.

In addition, in recognition of the number of students with mental health needs, a large percentage of schools have created clinics that offer psychological and psychiatric services. During the 2004–2005 academic year the official tally of such facilities stood at about 1,709, which was more than triple the number a decade earlier. Approximately 42 percent of these centers also provide violence-prevention education. One strategy such facilities implement is creating programs that help monitor and control bullying in the classroom.

In fact, in the decade following Columbine, many schools instituted zero-tolerance policies regarding social ostracizing and related aggression. The faculty at these institutions is committed to investigating any alleged episodes of bullying or fighting and to closely monitoring the social culture among the student body. The idea is to prevent bullying or harassment from becoming an accepted part of day-to-day life, as many sources allege it was at Columbine. Taking matters a step further, several federal lobbyists are in the process of promoting actual antibullying legislation. A handful of states has already adopted these laws, which essentially require local school boards to seriously address social issues such as harassment, fighting, and intolerance.

The work of organizations such as Safe School Ambassadors represents yet another approach to tackling this range of topics. The group was established by Community Matters in 2000 and, as of 2009, had advised staff at more than 650 schools across the country on how to deal with cliques and issues of ostracizing and aggression. As part of the program, faculty members are trained to communicate with leaders of various social groups within a particular school. In turn, these student representatives, or "ambassadors," cooperate to solve problems that arise as a result of bullying, as well as to keep adults and other authority figures aware of possible threats of violence.

If hints of a potential rampage do emerge, many schools currently have a police presence on-site or are at least prepared to be in immediate contact with local authorities to evaluate the situation promptly. In addition, specialized threat-assessment teams that are kept apprised of the latest research provided by the FBI, the U.S. Secret Service, and the U.S. Department of Education are often called in to analyze the nature and validity of the threat in question. Yet, even with such active involvement by the authorities, Phillips's opinion is that the key to preventing school violence is fostering open communication and an accepting social atmosphere.

"There has been an overemphasis by schools on an 'outside-in' approach that focuses heavily on security, crisis management, and punitive measures," he noted in 2009. "What is needed [instead] is an 'inside-out' approach that focuses on strengthening relationships and actively empowering young people to improve the school climate and change social norms. . . . Bullying continues to be a major factor leading to violence. Schools need to reach out to all students [and] particularly marginalized students.

They must empower and equip these young people with the skills, support, and opportunities to intervene effectively among their peers to reduce bullying and violence and to improve school climate."

While few people would dismiss measures intended to reduce bullying in schools, not everyone believes that such efforts have been a complete success. In the opinion of students and parents whose children continue to face social harassment at institutions that boast rigorous antibullying policies, sometimes the best-laid plans don't transform into realities. A 2008 study that profiled seventy-five schools and community centers in Colorado revealed that about 58 percent of students admitted to "either engaging in physical bullying or standing by while someone else did it." In addition, 67 percent of the individuals interviewed confessed to committing or tolerating verbal abuse.

"Bullying is still a significant problem in Colorado schools and schools nationally," said Elliott during a 2009 interview. "Very often teachers and principals don't have a good handle on how much bullying is going on." Tia Jones, who attends East High School in Denver, concurred with this assessment when asked to offer a student's perspective. The teenager has participated in programs designed to abate bullying but is not convinced that such prevention strategies are the answer.

"There [is] still bullying, fighting, [and] calling people names," Jones explained. "If you tell, you're a tattletale or a snitch." Though students at other schools across the country have described more positive results from antibullying initiatives, most experts agree that much work remains to be done if the cliquish and socially intolerant atmosphere that pervaded Columbine is to be avoided in schools nationwide.

"Over the ten years since Columbine, I've seen positive change," declared William Pollack, director of the National Violence Prevention and Study Center (NVPSC), a decade after the Littleton massacre. "But I still see too many tears and heartache and loss to feel that we're there and that we can give up the struggle. We're still in the middle of it."

Remembrance and Renewal

April 20, 2009, was marked by an intense wave of feelings and memories. It was a moment when millions of Americans paused, recalled the past, and reflected on the future. Tears were shed for loved ones lost ten years earlier, and the determination to fight school violence was renewed and strengthened.

At Clement Park, which is adjacent to Columbine, about a thousand people came together to participate in a memorial ceremony at sunset. In Denver crowds lobbied at the state capitol for stricter gun-control laws. And in the homes and workplaces of the men and women who survived Harris's and Klebold's rampage or were forced to bid farewell to family and friends too early as a result of it, there were varied reactions. These ranged from a need to know that loved ones did not die in vain to an appreciation for how even tragedy can shape an individual's perspective and future for the better.

"People have been able to have ten years to reconcile what happened and see what fits in their life and who they are," observed Kristi Mohrbacher of Littleton, who was a student attending Columbine when the massacre took place. "It's

Victims of the Columbine massacre were honored at Columbine Memorial Park on April 20, 2009.

kind of a part of who I am today. I think my priorities might be a little bit different if I hadn't had that experience."

Despite how life-altering the shooting was, however, many men and women connected to the killing noted that Harris and Klebold hadn't succeeded in changing everything. "They did not kill [their victims'] spirits," declared Tom Mauser, whose son was slain by the pair. "They did not kill our spirits either." Nor are the social issues brought to light by the tragedy likely to disappear any time soon. As proof of this, one needs only look to the myriad ways in

Triumph over Tragedy

On April 20, 2009, Colorado legislators passed a resolution on the floor of the state house of representatives. Titled "Triumph over Tragedy," or HJR09-1019, it drew national attention to the way the nation has responded to death and despair with change and progress. Portions of the resolution read as follows:

Whereas, April 20, 1999, was a day that forever changed not only Colorado but an entire nation; a day on which the Columbine High School community, the state of Colorado, and the nation as a whole suffered the tragic loss of innocence; and whereas, April 20, 1999, became a 'new beginning' for countless families and others who recognized this tragedy as a benchmark for change; and whereas, in the ten years since the tragedy at Columbine High School, efforts have been made throughout Colorado and the nation to understand how this tragedy happened and to prevent similar tragedies from occurring. . . . Be it resolved by the House of Representatives of the sixty-seventh general assembly of the state of Colorado, the senate concurring herein: That we, the members of the sixty-seventh general assembly of the state of Colorado, remember and honor those innocent victims who were killed, injured, or affected by the Columbine High School tragedy . . . [and] that we recognize and commend the individual and group efforts of the Columbine High School community in turning this tragedy into a triumph."

which people from lawmakers to moviemakers have recalled and referenced Columbine since April 20, 1999. Director Michael Moore's 2002 documentary *Bowling for Columbine* won an Academy Award for its in-depth look at gun violence in America, and Gus Van Sant's 2003 film *Elephant* offered a fictional portrayal of a remarkably similar school rampage at an otherwise ordinary U.S. high school.

In addition to these cinematic efforts, scores of writers have offered up books related to the Littleton shooting as well as countless theories about the perpetrators, their motives, and ways society can prevent such incidents. Meanwhile, local, state, and national politicians have voiced differing opinions on issues brought to light by Columbine, from gun-control laws to antibullying legislation. Regardless of their sometimes conflicting perspectives on these topics, the majority of lawmakers agree that the massacre should not only be a source of painful remembrances but also serve as an impetus for discussion, growth, and change.

According to Colorado state representative Ken Summers, such an attitude will help ensure "that Columbine will not just become a metaphor for tragedy but will show that we can triumph over the worst of humanity." To date, the term *Columbine* indeed invokes all that Summers expressed. Memories of the carnage have given way to serious contemplation and positive developments. Change has emerged in the form of heightened tolerance among high school cliques and increased communication among U.S. congressmembers on who should be allowed to purchase guns.

While school violence still shatters lives and forces the nation to recall the worst emotions the word *Columbine* stirs, it is an epidemic that men, women, and children across the United States are committed to ending. Their perspectives on this issue reflect the ideas and vantage points of everyone from run-of-the-mill teenagers to expert psychologists, but they all encompass a determination to make April 20, 1999, about far more than murder and mayhem in the classroom.

Timeline

1995   Harris and Klebold begin attending Columbine.

1997–1998   Harris and Klebold allegedly join the Trench Coat Mafia.

1997–1999   Klebold keeps a journal featuring personal thoughts that range from violent to romantic to depressive in nature.

January 1998   Harris and Klebold are arrested when they burglarize a van and steal approximately $400 worth of electronics. Brown's parents approach Jefferson County authorities to report suspicious and threatening messages on Harris's webpage.

December 1998   Harris and Klebold begin illegally obtaining firearms from older friends and acquaintances.

April 11, 1999   Harris mentions in one of several homemade videos that his parents are not to blame for his impending actions.

April 20, 1999   Harris and Klebold claim the lives of thirteen victims and wound twenty-three others before taking their own lives.

April 21, 1999   A bomb squad officially declares Columbine High School safe, and the bodies of those killed the day before are removed from the building.

April 22, 1999   President Clinton addresses the nation regarding Columbine and encourages people to reflect on the causes of school violence.

Summer 1999   The FBI's National Center for the Analysis of Violent Crime holds a conference to address school shootings.

2000   Psychologists Anderson and Dill publish a study that correlates violent video games to aggressive behavior in people who play them. Patti Nielson, who was injured by Harris and Klebold during their rampage, lobbies in Washington, D.C., for stricter gun-control laws. Community Matters establishes the Safe School Ambassadors program.

March 2002   Judge Babcock dismisses a lawsuit filed by family members of the Columbine victims and various individuals injured in the shooting against the manufacturers of violent video games.

2004–2005   The official number of schools that offer clinics with mental health services stands at about 1,709, more than triple the number from a decade earlier.

2005   The computer game *Super Columbine Massacre RPG!* becomes available online, allowing players to reenact the Columbine massacre from the perspective of the killers.

September 14, 2006   Atkinson alerts school officials at Green Bay East to threats of a shooting made by his friend Sturtz. Sturtz, Cornell, and Netwal are arrested shortly thereafter, leaving authorities to conclude that another Columbine was successfully averted.

2007   A report issued by the NCES and the BJS indicates that there have been approximately 50 percent fewer deaths per year related to school violence than in the seven years before the Columbine massacre.

April 16, 2007   Cho kills thirty-two people during his rampage at Virginia Tech. This same month, Judge Babcock seals records of testimony given by the Harris and Klebold families for a period of twenty years.

2008   A study profiling seventy-five schools and community centers in Colorado reveals that about 58 percent of students admit to having committed acts of physical bullying or having stood by while someone else did. Sixty-seven percent of the individuals interviewed also confess to engaging in or tolerating verbal abuse.

May 2008   A report issued by the U.S. Secret Service and the U.S. Department of Education details why many students fail to report threats of school violence made by their peers.

2009 A study conducted by Community Matters gives the country a grade of D+ in terms of school violence prevention. The group's Safe School Ambassadors program discloses that it has advised staff at more than 650 schools across the country on how to deal with cliques and issues of ostracizing and aggression.

April 20, 2009 Americans commemorate the tenth anniversary of the Columbine massacre. Colorado legislators pass a resolution titled "Triumph over Tragedy" that draws national attention to the way in which Columbine, the community of Littleton, and the nation have responded to the death and despair of April 20, 1999, with change and progress.

Notes

Chapter One

p. 9, ". . . a girl came running down the hall . . .": Nicole Nowlen, "My Story." 26 April 2009. NicoleNowlen.com. <http://www.nicolenowlen.com/> (Accessed 26 April 2009).

p. 13, ". . . not longer possible to . . .": Glenn Muschert, quoted in "Ten Years Later, Columbine's Hold Remains Strong." 17 April 2009. Yahoo! News. <http://news.yahoo.com/s/ap/20090417/ap_on_re_us/columbine_anniversary> (Accessed 27 April 2009).

p. 16, "normal guy": Acquaintance of Eric Harris, quoted in "Eric David Harris." 25 April 2009. A Columbine Site. <http://acolumbinesite.com/eric.html> (Accessed 26 April 2009).

p. 16, "typical kid": Acquaintances of Eric Harris, quoted in "Eric David Harris."

p. 16, ". . . he was the greatest actor . . .": Jennifer LaPlante, quoted in "Columbine—Tragedy and Recovery: A Boy with Many Sides," by Bill Briggs and Jason Blevins. 2 May 1999. *The Denver Post*. <http://extras.denverpost.com/news/shot0502b.htm> (Accessed 26 April 2009).

p. 17, ". . . America pass through these . . .": verbiage of Columbine school motto, quoted in "Introduction," *American Youth Cultures*, Neil Campbell, au. New York: Routledge, 2004, p.18.

p. 17, ". . . outcasts, kids who didn't . . .": Brooks Brown's father, quoted in "Columbine—Tragedy and Recovery: A Boy with Many Sides."

p. 17, ". . . school of cliques and the athletes . . .": Brooks Brown's father, quoted in "Columbine—Tragedy and Recovery: A Boy with Many Sides."

p. 17, ". . . I want to kill everyone . . .": Eric Harris, "Eric Harris's Writing." 25 April 2009. A Columbine Site. <http://acolumbinesite.com/eric/writing.html> (Accessed 26 April 2009).

p. 17, ". . . Kill everything. . . . Kill everything.": Eric Harris, "Eric Harris's Writing."

p. 17, ". . . man strikes with absolute . . .": Dylan Klebold, "Dylan Klebold's Writing." 25 April 2009. A Columbine Site. <http://acolumbinesite.com/dylan/writing.html> (Accessed 26 April 2009).

p. 19, ". . . they were taunted and teased about . . .": Tiffany Typher, quoted in "Columbine — Tragedy and Recovery: A Boy with Many Sides."

p. 20, ". . . framework of society stands . . .": Dylan Klebold, "Dylan Klebold's Writing."

p. 22, ". . . potential for an . . .": Columbine dean of students, quoted in "Dylan Bennet Klebold." 25 April 2009. A Columbine Site. <http://acolumbinesite.com/dylan.html> (Accessed 26 April, 2009).

p. 22, ". . . violent, angry streak in these . . .": Columbine dean of students, quoted in "Dylan Bennet Klebold."

Chapter Two

p. 26, "Judgment Day: The Columbine Tapes." 20 December 1999. *Time*. <http://www.time.com/time/magazine/article/0,9171,992873-8,00.html> (Accessed 26 April 2009).

p. 26, ". . . Get up; 6:00: Meet at KS . . .": Eric Harris, "Eric Harris's Writing."

p. 27, ". . . I like you now . . .": Eric Harris, quoted in

"Columbine Survivor with Words for Virginia Students," Brooks Brown, 18 April 2007. NPR. <http://www. npr.org/templates/story/story.php?storyId=9658182> (Accessed 26 April 2009).

p. 28, ". . . go on to lose four friends . . .": Brooks Brown, "Columbine Survivor with Words for Virginia Students."

p. 31, ". . . what we always wanted . . .": one of the Columbine shooters, quoted in "The Columbine Report—Two Killers Rampaged as Six Officers Awaited Aid," Mark Obmascik and David Olinger, 16 May 2000. *The Denver Post*. <http://extras.denverpost.com/news/col0516a.htm> (Accessed 29 April 2009).

p. 31, ". . . this report establishes a record . . .": Jefferson County investigators, quoted in "The Columbine Report— Two Killers Rampaged as Six Officers Awaited Aid."

p. 33, ". . . got every student in the library . . .": Patti Nielson and 911 dispatcher, "Columbine Student's 911 Call Transcript." Date last updated not available. A Columbine Site. <http://acolumbinesite.com/911/patti. html> (Accessed 26 April 2009).

p. 34, "All the jocks stand up . . .": one of the Columbine killers, quoted in "Dissecting Columbine's Cult of the Athlete," Lorraine Adams and Dale Russakoff, 12 June 1999. *The Washington Post*. <http://www.washingtonpost. com/wp-srv/national/daily/june99/columbine12.htm> (Accessed 30 April 2009).

p. 34, ". . . with a white hat or . . .": one of the Columbine killers, quoted in "Dissecting Columbine's Cult of the Athlete."

Chapter Three

p. 41, ". . . worst example of school violence . . .": Bill Clinton, "Clinton on School Violence." 22 April 1999. PBS *News Hour*. <http://www.pbs.org/newshour/bb/education/jan-june99/clinton_4-22.html> (Accessed 26 April 2009).

p. 42, ". . . parents I have ever . . .": Eric Harris, "Basement Tapes—First Tape: April 11, 1999." Date last updated not available. A Columbine Site. <http://acolumbinesite.com/quotes3.html> (Accessed 26 April 2009).

p. 42, ". . . nothing you guys could have done . . .": Eric Harris, "Basement Tapes—First Tape: April 11, 1999."

p. 43, ". . . not 'either/or' but 'both/and'. . .": Chad Dion Lassiter, "Interview with Chad Dion Lassiter, president of Black Men at Penn School of Social Work at the University of Pennsylvania," 17 April 2009.

p. 44, ". . . he suffered horribly . . .": Susan Klebold, quoted in "Forgiveness Not Needed, Say Klebold's Parents." 16 May 2004. MSNBC. <http://www.msnbc.msn.com/id/4990167> (Accessed 26 April 2009).

p. 44, "toxic culture": the Klebolds, quoted in "Forgiveness Not Needed, Say Klebold's Parents."

p. 44, ". . . saw how afraid and scared . . .": Patti Stevens, quoted in "Columbine Bullying No Myth, Panel Told," Howard Pankratz, 3 October 2000. *The Denver Post*. <http://extras.denverpost.com/news/col1003a.htm> (Accessed 26 April 2009).

p. 44, ". . . don't have those problems . . .": Frank DeAngelis, quoted in "Columbine Bullying No Myth, Panel Told."

p. 45, ". . . was not being reported . . .": Frank DeAngelis, quoted in "Witnesses Tell of Columbine Bullying," Jeff Kass. 3 October 2000. *Rocky Mountain News*. <http://denver.rockymountainnews.com/shooting/1003col4.shtml> (Accessed 26 April 2009).

p. 45, ". . . why did he show up at . . .": Frank DeAngelis, quoted in "Columbine Bully Talk Persists," Holly Kurtz, 26 August 2000. *Rocky Mountain News*.

p. 45, ". . . were students who worked . . .": Devon Adams, quoted in "Columbine Bully Talk Persists."

p. 46, "playing out their game in God mode": investigator who worked on the Columbine case, quoted in "Video Games and Aggressive Thoughts, Feelings, and Behavior in the Laboratory and in Life," Craig Anderson and Karen Dill. (Specific date last updated not available) 2008. *Journal of Personality and Social Psychology*. <http://www.apa.org/journals/features/psp784772.pdf> (Accessed 26 April 2009).

p. 46, ". . . media affects our lives . . .": Craig Anderson and Karen Dill, "Video Games and Aggressive Thoughts, Feelings, and Behavior in the Laboratory and in Life."

p. 48, ". . . combination of extremely violent video games . . .": verbiage of lawsuit filed against video-game manufacturers in wake of Columbine, quoted in "Columbine Families Sue Computer Game Makers," Mark Ward, 1 May 2001. BBC News. <http://news.bbc.co.uk/1/hi/sci/tech/1295920.stm> (Accessed 26 April 2009).

p. 49, ". . . that there is social utility . . .": Lewis Babcock, quoted in "Columbine Lawsuit Against Makers of

Video Games, Movies Thrown Out." 5 March 2002. The Freedom Forum. <http://www.freedomforum. org/templates/document.asp?documentID=15820> (Accessed 26 April 2009).

p. 49, "We all know that we've watched . . .": Douglas Gentile, quoted in "Psychologists Explore Public Policy and Effects of Media Violence on Children." 27 December 2007. *Science Daily.* <http://www.sciencedaily. com/releases/2007/12/071221134342.htm> (Accessed 26 April 2009).

p. 50, ". . . been living with Columbine for . . .": Brooks Brown, quoted in "Shock, Anger Over Columbine Video Game," Jose Antonio Vargas. 20 May 2006. *The Washington Post.* <http://www.washingtonpost.com/wp-dyn/content/ article/2006/05/19/AR2006051901979.html> (Accessed 29 April 2009).

p. 51, ". . . not advocating shooting up . . .": Danny Ledonne, quoted in "Shock, Anger Over Columbine Video Game."

Chapter Four

p. 52, ". . . one can ever say . . .": Frank DeAngelis, quoted in "Lessons from Columbine: More Security, Outreach in Schools," Gregg Toppo and Marilyn Elias, 13 Apr. 2009. *USA Today.* <http://www.usatoday.com/news/ education/2009-04-13-columbine-lessons_N.htm> (Accessed 26 April 2009).

p. 53, ". . . a dealer told them that they needed . . .": Robyn Anderson, quoted in "S4057." 17 May 2000.

Congressional Record—Senate. <http://bulk.resource. org/gpo.gov/record/2000/2000_S04057.pdf> (Accessed 26 April 2009).

p. 54, ". . . person must be twenty-one years . . .": verbiage of federal laws related to the purchase and possession of firearms, "Age Restrictions on the Purchase and Possession of Firearms." 28 October 1999. The National Rifle Association Institute for Legislative Action. <http:// www.nraila.org/Issues/factsheets/read.aspx?ID=43> (Accessed 26 April 2009).

p. 56, ". . . not become an activist . . .": Patti Nielsen, quoted in "Columbine Survivor Speaks for Gun Control," Michael Romano, 6 April 2000. *Rocky Mountain News*. <http:// denver.rockymountainnews.com/shooting/0406lib3. shtml> (Accessed 26 April 2009).

p. 56, ". . . crackdown would have prevented . . .": Dave Kopel, "Getting Columbine Right." 12 October 2000. The Second Amendment Project. <http://www. davekopel.com/NRO/2000/Getting-Columbina-Right. htm> (Accessed 26 April 2009).

p. 57, ". . . shattered any remaining hopes . . .": Janalee Tobias, "Columbine Was an Easy Target—Guns Protect Schools from Criminals." 20 April 2009. *U.S. News and World Report*. <http://www.usnews.com/articles/opinion/2009/04/20/ columbine-was-an-easy-target—guns-protect-schools- from-criminals.html> (Accessed 29 April 2009).

p. 59, ". . . got some information about some kids . . .": Jefferson County investigators, quoted in "Could Columbine

Have Been Prevented?" 11 April 2001. CBS News. <http://www.cbsnews.com/stories/2001/04/07/national/main284525.shtml> (Accessed 26 April 2009).

p. 59, ". . . every high school in the country . . .": Jefferson County investigators, quoted in "Could Columbine Have Been Prevented?"

p. 59, "great details": Dylan Klebold's English teacher, quoted in "Columbine—Klebold Essay Foretold Columbine, Chillingly," Howard Pankratz, 22 November 2000. *The Denver Post.* <http://extras.denverpost.com/news/col1003a.htm> (Accessed 26 April 2009).

p. 59, ". . .to understand kids these . . .": the Klebolds, quoted in "Columbine—Klebold Essay Foretold Columbine, Chillingly."

p. 61, ". . . cannot afford to not follow up . . .": Harry Trombitas, quoted in "Lethal Hints—Red Flags Suggest Which Students Will Become School Shooters, Experts Say," Martin Rosenman, 6 July 2008. *The Columbus Dispatch.* <http://74.125.95.132/search?q=cache:bUWXkD1Lq-YJ:www.osroa.org/mediakit/lethalweapons.pdf+columbine+preventable+take+hints+of+violence+seriously&cd=1&hl=en&ct=clnk&gl=us> (Accessed 26 April 2009).

p. 61, ". . . threats are not created . . .": attendees at the 1999 conference hosted by the FBI's National Center for the Analysis of Violent Crime to address school shootings, "Student Threat Assessment as a Strategy to Reduce School Violence," *The Handbook of School Violence and School Safety: From Research to Practice*, Shane

R. Jimerson and Michael J. Furlong, eds. New York: Routledge, 2006, p. 588.

p. 61, ". . . the use of student profiling . . .": FBI profiling experts, quoted in "Student Threat Assessment as a Strategy to Reduce School Violence," p. 587.

p. 62, ". . . other people concerned about . . .": Eleven Questions to Aid Data Collection in a Threat Assessment Inquiry, *Department of Education and United States Secret Service Threat Assessment Guide*. Date last updated not available. Positive Environments, Network of Trainers (PENT): California Department of Education. <http://www.pent.ca.gov/threat.htm> (Accessed 16 June 2009).

p. 64, ". . . who is wearing black is a . . .": Allan Garcia, quoted in "Middletown Police Prepare for Worst-Case Scenario." (Specific date last updated not available.) Matt Sheley, 2007. School Violence Solutions. <http://www. schoolviolencesolutions.com/news.html> (Accessed 26 April 2009).

Chapter Five

p. 66, ". . . vandalized my heart, raped my . . .": Seung-Hui Cho, quoted in "NBC Defends Release of Virginia Tech Gunman Video," Howard Berkes, Barbara Bradley Hagerty, and Jennifer Ludden. 19 April 2007. NPR. <http://www.npr.org/templates/story/story.php?storyId=9604204> (Accessed 27 April 2009).

p. 66, "martyrs like Eric and Dylan": Seung-Hui Cho, quoted in "Ten Years Later, Columbine's Hold Remains Strong."

p. 68, ". . . hate it when people say . . .": Patrick Ireland, quoted in "Ten Years Later, Columbine's Hold Remains Strong."

p. 69, ". . . iconic shooting. It defined . . .": Katherine S. Newman, quoted in "Ten Years Later, Columbine's Hold Remains Strong."

p. 69, ". . . my thoughts went back to . . .": Frank DeAngelis, "Columbine Families Mourn Virginia Tech." 20 April 2007. CBS News. <http://www.cbsnews.com/stories/2007/04/20/columbine/main2709495.shtml> (Accessed 27 April 2009).

p. 69, ". . . felt like I was looking at Lauren's . . .": Dawn Anna, "Columbine Families Mourn Virginia Tech." 20 April 2007. CBS News. <http://www.cbsnews.com/stories/2007/04/20/columbine/main2709495.shtml> (Accessed 27 April 2009).

p. 71, ". . . don't think you can stop every crazy . . .": Don Fleming, "Columbine Families Mourn Virginia Tech."

p. 71, ". . . deprives the rest of the country . . .": Katherine S. Newman, "Columbine Families Mourn Virginia Tech."

p. 73, ". . . want this period of time . . .": Tony Sherman, "NBC Exec: Airing Cho Video 'Good Journalism'." 24 April 2007. MSNBC. <http://www.msnbc.msn.com/id/18295682/> (Accessed 29 April 2009).

p. 73, ". . . close as we'll ever come . . .": Steve Capus, quoted in "NBC Defends Release of Virginia Tech Gunman Video."

p. 73, ". . . good journalism is bad . . .": Steve Capus, quoted in "NBC President Defends Decision to Air Video of

Virginia Tech Shooter." 24 April 2007. *The Arkansas Democrat Gazette.* <http://www2.arkansasonline.com/news/2007/apr/24/nbc-president-defends-decision-air-video-virginia-/> (Accessed 29 April 2009).

p. 74, ". . . there have been copycat events . . .": Del Elliott, "Columbine Not Ceding Its Secrets." 14 February 2007. *The Denver Post.* <http://www.denverpost.com/columbine/ci_5221781> (Accessed 27 April 2009).

p. 76, "shoot the place up": Shawn Sturtz, quoted in "Three Wisconsin Teens Charged in Planned School-Shooting Plot." 22 September 2006. Fox News. <http://www.foxnews.com/story/0,2933,215145,00.html> (Accessed 27 April 2009).

p. 76, ". . . what do you mean . . .": Matt Atkinson and Shawn Sturtz, quoted in "Three Wisconsin Teens Charged in Planned School-Shooting Plot."

p. 77, ". . . a Columbine waiting to . . .": John Zakowski, quoted in "This Was a Columbine Waiting to Happen." 27 April 09. *The Green Bay Press Gazette.* <http://www.greenbaypressgazette.com/article/99999999/GPG0101/609150615/0/specials01> (Accessed 27 April 2009).

p. 77, ". . . statements that we heard . . .": Craig Van Schyndle, quoted in "This Was a Columbine Waiting to Happen."

p. 77, ". . . decided it was my duty . . .": Matt Atkinson, quoted in "'I Decided It Was My Duty to Inform the Authorities,' East Student Says." 27 April 2009. *The Green Bay Press Gazette.* <http://www.greenbaypressgazette.com/

article/99999999/GPG0101/609210543/0/specials01>
(Accessed 27 April 2009).

p. 77, ". . . believe there were probably other people . . .":
Tom Molitor, quoted in "Police Stop Wisconsin Shooting
Attack." 15 September 2006. CBS3. <http://cbs3.
com/topstories/Green.Bay.Wisconsin.2.272654.html>
(Accessed 27 April 2009).

p. 78, ". . . to believe [a school shooting] . . .": student #1
interviewed for report issued by the U.S. Secret Service
and U.S. Department of Education in May 2008, "Prior
Knowledge of Potential School-Based Violence—
Information Students Learn May Prevent a Targeted
Attack," *Appendix: Case Studies.* (Specific date last updated
not available) May 2008. The United States Secret
Service and the United States Department of Education.
<http://ustreas.gov/usss/ntac/bystander_study.pdf>
(Accessed 27 April 2009).

p. 78, "had everything under control": student #2 interviewed
for report issued by the U.S. Secret Service and U.S.
Department of Education in May 2008, "Prior Knowledge
of Potential School-Based Violence—Information
Students Learn May Prevent a Targeted Attack."

p. 78, ". . . might have thought twice . . .": student #3
interviewed for report issued by the U.S. Secret Service
and U.S. Department of Education in May 2008, "Prior
Knowledge of Potential School-Based Violence—
Information Students Learn May Prevent a Targeted
Attack."

Chapter Six

p. 81, ". . . think that a school shooter . . .": Gary Rose, "Anniversary of Columbine Has Area Schools Reflecting on Need for Security." 20 April 2009. *Democrat and Chronicle.* <http://www.democratandchronicle.com/article/20090420/NEWS01/904200334> (Accessed 27 April 2009).

p. 82, ". . . been about half as many . . .": verbiage of a 2007 report from the National Center for Education Statistics and the Bureau of Justice Statistics, quoted in "Columbine Massacre Changed School Security."

p. 83, ". . . a careful review of existing school violence . . .": "Ten Years After Columbine: Nation Earns D+ on School Violence-Prevention." 16 April 2009. PR Newswire Association LLC. <http://news.prnewswire.com/DisplayReleaseContent.aspx?ACCT=104&STORY=/www/story/04-16-2009/0005007032&EDATE=> (Accessed 27 April 2009).

p. 83, ". . . is not an indictment of any . . .": Rick Phillips, quoted in "Ten Years After Columbine: Nation Earns D+ on School Violence-Prevention."

p. 84, ". . . after any of these incidents . . .": William Modzeleski, quoted in "Columbine Massacre Changed School Security," John D. Stutter. 20 April 2009. CNN. <http://www.cnn.com/2009/LIVING/04/20/columbine.school.safety/index.html> (Accessed 27 April 2009).

p. 84, ". . . can check the guns at the door . . .": Rick Phillips, quoted in "Ten Years after Columbine High Massacre, Are Dallas-Fort Worth Schools Any Safer? It's Hard to

Say," Holly K. Hacker and Tawnell D. Hobbs. 18 April 2009. *The Dallas Morning News.* <http://www.dallasnews.com/sharedcontent/dws/news/city/collin/plano/stories/041909dnmcolumbineanniversary_19met.State.Edition1.3e6dc43.html> (Accessed 27 April 2009).

p. 86, ". . . an overemphasis by schools . . .": Rick Phillips, quoted in "Ten Years after Columbine: Nation Earns D+ on School Violence-Prevention."

p. 87, ". . . engaging in physical bullying . . .": results of 2008 study that profiled seventy-five schools and community centers in Colorado, quoted in "Bullies Still Lurking in School Halls," Colleen O'Connor, 19 April 2009. *The Denver Post.* <http://www.denverpost.com/ci_12174189> (Accessed 27 April 2009).

p. 87, ". . . still a significant problem . . .": Del Elliott, quoted in "Bullies Still Lurking in School Halls."

p. 87, ". . . [is] still bullying, fighting . . .": Tia Jones, quoted in "Bullies Still Lurking in School Halls."

p. 88, ". . . the ten years since Columbine . . .": William Pollack, quoted in "Bullies Still Lurking in School Halls."

p. 88, ". . . have been able to have ten years . . .": Kristi Mohrbacher, quoted in "Columbine Massacre Survivors Push Ahead." 20 April 2009. MSNBC. <http://www.msnbc.msn.com/id/30294427/> (Accessed 27 April 2009).

p. 89, ". . . did not kill [their victims'] . . .": Tom Mauser, quoted in "Words of Healing on Tenth Anniversary of Columbine." 20 April 2009. ABC7 — The Denver Channel. <http://www.thedenverchannel.com/news/19231148/detail.html>. (Accessed 27 April 2009)

p. 90, ". . . was a day that forever changed . . .": verbiage of "Triumph over Tragedy" resolution, "HJR09-1019." 20 April 2009. First Regular Session—Sixty Seventh General Assembly: State of Colorado. <http://www.leg.state.co.us/Clics/CLICS2009A/csl.nsf/fsbillcont3/F6F41240D9B73846872575780056CAB2?Open&file=HJR1019_01.pdf> (Accessed 29 April 2009).

p. 92, ". . . will not just become a . . .": Ken Summers, quoted in "Columbine Has Triumphed Over Tragedy, Lawmakers Say," John Ingold. 20 April 2009. *The Denver Post.* <http://www.denverpost.com/breakingnews/ci_12183773?source=rss> (Accessed 27 April 2009).

Further Information

Books

Burns, Kate (editor). *School Violence.* Farmington Hills, MI: Greenhaven Press, 2005.

Keuss, Jeff, and Lia Sloth. *Rachel's Challenge: A Columbine Legacy.* Kirkland, WA: Positively for Kids, 2006.

Lindholm, Marjorie, and Peggy Lindholm. *A Columbine Survivor's Story.* Littleton, CO: Regenold Publishing, 2005.

DVDs

Bowling for Columbine. Dir. Michael Moore. Alliance Atlantis Communications, 2003.

Elephant. Dir. Gus Van Sant. Perf. Alex Frost, Eric Deulen. HBO Films, 2004.

Websites

A Columbine Site
http://acolumbinesite.com/
This site features a comprehensive overview of the people and events related to April 20, 1999, as well as several photographs, online documents, and video and audio clips.

CNN—Jefferson County, Colorado, Sheriff: Columbine Time Lines
www.cnn.com/SPECIALS/2000/columbine.cd/Pages/TOC.htm
This site contains detailed timelines, narrative information, and audio clips connected to the Columbine massacre.

National Youth Violence Prevention Resource Center — School Violence

www.safeyouth.org/scripts/topics/school.asp

This site includes a wide array of facts and statistics related to school violence, as well as a selection of strategies on how to cope with and prevent it.

Bibliography

Adams, Lorraine, and Dale Russakoff. "Dissecting Columbine's Cult of the Athlete." *The Washington Post*, June 12, 1999. www.washingtonpost.com/wp-srv/national/daily/june99/columbine12.htm.

Anderson, Craig A. and Karen E. Dill. "Video Games and Aggressive Thoughts, Feelings, and Behavior in the Laboratory and in Life," *Journal of Personality and Social Psychology*, 2000, Vol. 78, No. 4, pp. 772–790. www.apa.org/journals/features/psp784772.pdf.

Berkes, Howard, Barbara Bradley Hagerty, and Jennifer Ludden. "NBC Defends Release of Virginia Tech Gunman Video," NPR, April 18, 2007. www.npr.org/templates/story/story.php?storyId=9604204.

Bowling for Columbine. Dir. Michael Moore. 2002. Alliance Atlantis Communications.

Briggs, Bill and David Blevins. "Columbine—Tragedy and Recovery: A Boy with Many Sides," *The Denver Post*, May 2, 1999. http://extras.denverpost.com/news/shot0502b.htm.

Brown, Brooks. "Columbine Survivor with Words for Virginia Students," NPR, April 18, 2007. www.npr.org/templates/story/story.php?storyId=9658182.

Campbell, Neil. *American Youth Cultures.* New York: Routledge, 2004.

Clinton, William. "Clinton on School Violence," transcript of discussion with four teachers on April 22, 1999. PBS

NewsHour. www.pbs.org/newshour/bb/education/jan-june99/clinton_4-22.html.

"Columbine Lawsuit Against Makers of Video Games, Movies Thrown Out," Freedom Forum, March 5, 2002. www.freedomforum.org/templates/document.asp?documentID=15820.

"Columbine Massacre Survivors Push Ahead," MSNBC, April 20, 2009. www.msnbc.msn.com/id/30294427.

"Columbine Student's 911 Call Transcript," A Columbine Site, April 20, 1999. http://acolumbinesite.com/911/patti.html.

"Could Columbine Have Been Prevented?" CBS News, April 11, 2001. www.cbsnews.com/stories/2001/04/07/national main284525.shtml.

Cullen, Dave. *Columbine*. New York: Twelve, 2009.

Department of Education and United States Secret Service. "Threat Assessment Guide." Positive Environments; Network of Trainers — California Department of Education. www.pent.ca.gov/threat.htm.

De Vries, Lloyd. "Columbine Families Mourn Virginia Tech," CBS News, April 20, 2007. www.cbsnews.com/stories/2007/04/20/columbine/main2709495.shtml.

"Dylan Bennet Klebold," A Columbine Site. http://acolumbinesite.com/dylan.html.

"Dylan Klebold's Writing," A Columbine Site. http://acolumbinesite.com/dylan/writing.html.

Elephant. Dir. Gus Van Sant. Perf. Alex Frost, Eric Deulen. 2003. HBO Films.

"Eric David Harris," A Columbine Site. http://acolumbinesite.com/eric.html.

"Eric Harris's Writing," A Columbine Site. http://acolumbinesite.com/eric/writing.html.

"Forgiveness Not Needed, Say Klebold's Parents," MSNBC, May 16, 2004. www.msnbc.msn.com/id/4990167.

Gibbs, Nancy, Timothy Roche, Andrew Goldstein, Maureen Harrington, and Richard Woodbury. "The Columbine Tapes," *Time*, December 20, 1999. www.time.com/time/magazine/article/0,9171,992873-8,00.html.

Hacker, Holly and Tawnell D. Hobbs. "Ten Years After Columbine High Massacre, Are Dallas-Fort Worth Schools Any Safer? It's Hard to Say," *The Dallas Morning News*, April 18, 2009. www.dallasnews.com/sharedcontent/dws/news/city/collin/plano/stories/041909dnmcolumbineanniversary_19met.State.Edition1.3e6dc43.html

Harris, Eric and Dylan Klebold. "Basement Tapes: First Tape—April 11, 1999," A Columbine Site. http://acolumbinesite.com/quotes3.html.

Hurtz, Holly. "Columbine Bully Talk Persists," *Rocky Mountain*

News, August 26, 2000. http://denver.rockymountainnews.com/shooting/0826colu3.shtml.

Ingold, John. "Columbine Has Triumphed Over Tragedy, Lawmakers Say," *The Denver Post*, April 20, 2009. www.denverpost.com/breakingnews/ci_12183773?source=rss.

Jefferson County, Colorado, Sheriff. "Columbine Time Lines," www.cnn.com/SPECIALS/2000/columbine.cd/Pages/TOC.htm.

Jimerson, Shane R., and Michael J. Furlong (editors). *The Handbook of School Violence and School Safety: From Research to Practice*. New York: Routledge, 2006.

Kass, Jeff. *Columbine: A True Crime Story*. Denver: Ghost Road Publishing Group, Inc., 2009.

Kass, Jeff. "Witnesses Tell of Columbine Bullying," *Rocky Mountain News*, October 3, 2000. http://denver.rockymountainnews.com/shooting/1003col4.shtml.

Kopel, Dave. "Getting Columbine Right," The Second Amendment Project, October 12, 2000. www.davekopel.com/NRO/2000/Getting-Columbina-Right.htm.

Larkin, Ralph W. *Comprehending Columbine*. Philadelphia: Temple University Press, 2007.

Lee, Nichole. "Anniversary of Columbine Has Area Schools Reflecting on Need for Security," *Democrat and Chronicle*, April 20, 2009. www.democratandchronicle.com/article/20090420/NEWS01/904200334.

Lindholm, Marjorie, and Peggy Lindholm. *A Columbine Survivor's Story*. Littleton, CO: Regenold Publishing, 2005.

Marsico, Katie. "Interview with Chad Dion Lassiter, president of Black Men at Penn School of Social Work at the University of Pennsylvania," April 17, 2009.

Mowlen, Nicole. "My Story." www.nicolenowlen.com/.

National Rifle Association Institute for Legislative Action. "Age Restrictions on the Purchase and Possession of Firearms," October 28, 1999. www.nraila.org/Issues/fact sheets/read.aspx?ID=43.

National Youth Violence Prevention Resource Center. "School Violence." www.safeyouth.org/scripts/topics/school.asp.

"NBC Exec: Airing Cho Video 'Good Journalism'," MSNBC, April 24, 2007. www.msnbc.msn.com/id/18295682/.

"NBC President Defends Decision to Air Video of Virginia Tech Shooter," *The Arkansas Democrat Gazette*, July 15, 2009. www2.arkansasonline.com/news/2007/apr/24/nbc-presi dent-defends-decision-air-video-virginia-/.

Obmascik, Mark and David Olinger. "The Columbine Report—Two Killers Rampaged as Six Officers Awaited Aid," *The Denver Post*, May 16, 2000. http://extras.denverpost. com/news/col0516a.htm.

O'Connor, Colleen. "Bullies Still Lurking in School Halls," *The Denver Post*, April 19, 2009. www.denverpost.com/ ci_12174189.

Pankratz, Howard. "Columbine Bullying No Myth, Panel Told," *The Denver Post*, October 3, 2000. http://extras.denverpost.com/news/col1003a.htm.

Pankratz, Howard. "Columbine—Klebold Essay Foretold Columbine, Chillingly," October 20, 2000, *The Denver Post*. http://extras.denverpost.com/news/col1003a.htm.

Phelps, Nathan. "'I Decided It Was My Duty to Inform the Authorities,' East Student Says," *The Green Bay Press Gazette*, July 15, 2009. www.greenbaypressgazette.com/article/99999999/GPG0101/609210543/0/specials01.

Phelps, Nathan. "This Was a Columbine Waiting to Happen," *The Green Bay Press Gazette*, July 15, 2009. www.greenbaypressgazette.com/article/99999999/GPG0101/609150615/0/specials01.

"Police Stop Wisconsin Shooting Attack," CBS3/Philly 57, September 15, 2006. http://cbs3.com/topstories/Green.Bay.Wisconsin.2.272654.html.

"Psychologists Explore Public Policy and Effects of Media Violence on Children," *Science Daily*, December 27, 2007. www.sciencedaily.com/releases/2007/12/071221134342.htm.

Rodriguez, Rachel, and Christina Zdanowicz. "Nothing the Same After Columbine, Say Students, Teachers," CNN, April 21, 2009. www.cnn.com/2009/US/04/20/columbine.irpt/index.html.

Romano, Michael. "Columbine Survivor Speaks for Gun Control," *Rocky Mountain News*, April 6, 2000. http://denver. rockymountainnews.com/shooting/0406lib3.shtml.

Rozenman, Martin. "Lethal Hints—Red Flags Suggest Which Students Will Become School Shooters, Experts Say," *The Columbus Dispatch*, July 6, 2008. http://74.125.95.132/ search?q=cache:bUWXkD1Lq-YJ:www.osroa.org/ mediakit/lethalweapons.pdf+columbine+preventable+take+ hints+of+violence+seriously&cd=1&hl=en&ct=clnk&gl=us.

Sheley, Matt. "Middletown Police Prepare for Worst-Case Scenario," School Violence Solutions. www. schoolviolencesolutions.com/news.html.

Sixty Seventh General Assembly: State of Colorado. "First Regular Session: HJR09-1019," www.leg.state.co.us/Clics/ CLICS2009A/csl.nsf/fsbillcont3/F6F41240D9B738468725 75780056CAB2?Open&file=HJR1019_01.pdf.

Spencer, Jim. "Columbine Not Ceding Its Secrets," *The Denver Post*, February 14, 2007. www.denverpost.com/ columbine/ci_5221781.

Sutter, John D. "Columbine Massacre Changed School Security," CNN, April 20, 2009. www.cnn.com/2009/ LIVING/04/20/columbine.school.safety/index.html.

"Ten Years After Columbine: Nation Earns D+ on School Violence-Prevention," PR Newswire Association

LLC, April 16, 2009. http://news.prnewswire.com/Display
ReleaseContent.aspx?ACCT=104&STORY=/www/
story/04-16-2009/0005007032&EDATE=.

"Ten Years Later, Columbine's Hold Remains Strong,"
Yahoo! News, April 19, 2009. http://news.yahoo.com/s/
ap/20090417/ap_on_re_us/columbine_anniversary.

"Three Wisconsin Teens Charged in Planned School-
Shooting Plot," Fox News, September 22, 2006. www.
foxnews.com/story/0,2933,215145,00.html.

Tobias, Janalee. "Columbine Was an Easy Target:
Guns Protect Schools from Criminals," *U.S. News and
World Report*, April 20, 2009. www.usnews.com/articles/
opinion/2009/04/20/columbine-was-an-easy-target—guns-
protect-schools-from-criminals.html.

Toppo, Greg and Marilyn Elias. "Lessons from Columbine:
More Security, Outreach in Schools," *USA Today*, April
13, 2009. www.usatoday.com/news/education/2009-04-13-
columbine-lessons_N.htm.

United States Secret Service and the United States
Department of Education. "Prior Knowledge of Potential
School-Based Violence: Information Students Learn May
Prevent a Targeted Attack," May 2008. http://ustreas.gov/
usss/ntac/bystander_study.pdf.

United States Senate. "Congressional Record S4057," May 17,
2000. http://bulk.resource.org/gpo.gov/record/2000/2000_
S04057.pdf.

Vargas, Jose Antonio. "Shock, Anger Over Columbine Video Game," *The Washington Post*, May 20, 2006. www.washingtonpost.com/wp-dyn/content/article/2006/05/19/AR2006051901979.html.

Ward, Mark. "Columbine Families Sue Computer Game Makers," BBC News, May 1, 2001. http://news.bbc.co.uk/1/hi/sci/tech/1295920.stm.

"Words of Healing on Tenth Anniversary of Columbine," The Denver Channel, April 20, 2009. www.thedenverchannel.com/news/19231148/detail.html.

Index

Page numbers in **boldface** are illustrations.

About the Author

KATIE MARSICO is the author of more than fifty reference books for children and young adults. Prior to becoming a full-time writer, Marsico worked as a managing editor in publishing. She resides near Chicago, Illinois, with her husband, daughter, and two sons.